FOUNDER BRAND

FOUNDER BRAND

TURN YOUR STORY INTO YOUR COMPETITIVE ADVANTAGE

DAVE GERHARDT

LIONCREST
PUBLISHING

FOUNDER BRAND
Turn Your Story Into Your Competitive Advantage

ISBN   978-1-5445-2341-5   *Hardcover*
978-1-5445-2340-8   *Paperback*
978-1-5445-2342-2   *Ebook*

CONTENTS

FOREWORD

by Hiten Shah

CEO OF NIRA.COM

I am Hiten Shah, CEO of Nira.com, where we focus on keeping your company's internal documents secure.

I have known and worked with Dave Gerhardt for six years. To understand why I would want to write the foreword for Dave's book, you have to understand how we came to collaborate, which happened because of Drift's founder David Cancel.

Prior to Drift, David Cancel was at HubSpot. We competed for the same clientele, and I quickly decided I would *never* compete against him again. Not because he was an aggressive competitor, but because he was so customer-centric that it would be hard for anyone to outdo him. I learned from his emphasis, but I knew I couldn't beat him at meeting the customer's needs.

Fast-forward to his starting Drift, and we connected again. He asked for advice on marketing, and I'd give my very blunt recommendations on how Drift should carve out their segment of the market.

Then Dave Gerhardt joined the Drift team, and the magic happened.

David Cancel asked me to talk through some of my thoughts with Dave. In our conversation, the idea of promoting David Cancel as the founder of Drift grew, as opposed to marketing the as-of-yet unknown products of Drift.

Dave internalized and then celebrated the idea that David Cancel was someone who people should hear from directly. Dave used his expertise in social media and in podcasting to take David's very clear message and profound knowledge and publish it into the world.

By taking the time to get to know David Cancel, Dave pulled the words and ideas out of David and used them to build the brand around him as Drift's founder.

Those of us in the field watched this journey unfold. People who followed David's journey developed trust and connection to him and Drift, meaning Drift had potential customers lined up waiting to buy their product when it launched. It was pure magic.

This model of developing the story of the founder and using that as the basis of building a founder brand was, and still is, brilliant. It is a simple, formulaic process, but one that has the potential to reap huge rewards for a company.

In the years that have passed since Dave's work at Drift, he has clarified and built out the founder brand framework to a point that he has replicated it with many other brands and teaches it in marketing classes at Harvard Business School.

At the heart of the Founder Brand is human connection, which we all crave. It allows us to feel we know the founder and the reasons for the brand. When we feel we have a relationship with someone leading a brand, we are more likely to try their products. This relatively simple model requires less effort than you would think, especially once you start practicing it on a consistent basis.

I'm convinced that the only way to build a successful, large company is to use Dave's founder brand framework.

Try it! It works.

INTRODUCTION

The goal of marketing is to make sales easier.

I say that because good marketing builds awareness, trust, and credibility. And having those things makes it much easier to sell your products and services to your dream customers when they need them.

Today, there are more ways than ever for businesses to do marketing. You can start a blog, a podcast, a newsletter, a YouTube channel, a Substack, a Patreon. You can be active on Twitter. And LinkedIn. And TikTok. You can speak at events. You can host events. You can do field marketing, channel marketing, and partner marketing. There are literally dozens of ways to market your business today.

But I've found one that is still overlooked and, most often, completely ignored.

It's a marketing strategy that I used to help Drift become one of the fastest growing SaaS companies of all time and achieve over a billion-dollar valuation. It's a marketing strategy that I used to help Privy get acquired by Attentive for nine figures.

And in this book, I'm going to do my best to share that marketing strategy with you: it's all about building a brand for the company's *founder*.

THE DRIFT STORY

When people start a new business, they often miss the most obvious and easy way to market it, which is to tell the founder's story. I see so many startups and new companies jump right into product features. And that's important—you have to market the product, of course. But at the end of the day, people buy from *people*, and building a brand for the founder is an incredible way to cut through the noise and build trust and credibility with potential customers in the early days of a company when you need every advantage you can get. This idea of focusing on the founder's story was revolutionary to me as a marketer at a startup personally—and it's worked time and time again, which is why now I'm here writing this book. Marketing is all about understanding people, and what I knew was that people like to know other people, but I hadn't fully comprehended the power of the connection being with the *founder*.

Shortly after I began working at Drift, I met with one of our advisors, Hiten Shah. We were kicking around ideas about how we might put Drift on the map (and I think he was doing a little bit of sizing me up on behalf of the Drift founders, of course). Hiten is a master of digital marketing and social media, especially when it comes to start-ups. And in our conversation, he pushed me on the idea of building a brand for David Cancel, the company's CEO and founder, instead of just pushing the Drift product.

David Cancel had a big following on Twitter already and was well known in the local startup and VC community, so we went out into the Boston area to get him booked for speaking events, podcast interviews, and guest blog posts. His Twitter following was important, because we were able to target our outreach to active and engaged members of that audience (a.k.a. people who already knew David). We used those connections to promote the idea of an innovative company in Boston; but we didn't just focus on the Drift product. We focused on telling David's story. He was the former Chief Product Officer at HubSpot, which had just gone public. He had a few successful startup exits before starting Drift. He was a frequent guest lecturer at top business schools like Harvard Business School and MIT. And he was building his *fifth* startup—all of which have been in a similar niche (sales and marketing technology). So as a marketer, I had a lot to work with outside of the company story. And then we launched his podcast, *Seeking Wisdom*, where each week he was on the mic, I got to play co-host, and we got to open up a bit more. Instead of just seeing tweets from David about his experience, people were able to hear him firsthand through the podcast. Each week we'd record new episodes where I'd interview David about his background, life, learnings, working style, startup lessons, and more. This allowed us to turn passive Twitter followers into raving podcast fans. Instead of just scrolling through Twitter and seeing David's tweets, we now had people literally listening to his voice in their headphones every week. As that podcast exploded (50,000 downloads/

month), we felt a direct impact on the attention and awareness for Drift too. Despite never pitching our products and services on the podcast directly, *Seeking Wisdom* became the number one reason people heard about Drift and eventually bought our products. It was because people got to know, like, and trust us through *Seeking Wisdom*, through David (and myself) being active on Twitter.

Now, I'd be lying if I said that I wasn't lucky. Not all startup founders and CEOs do this. They don't all want to start a podcast and be active on social media and go speak at events. Luckily for me and for Drift, David Cancel was a founder who truly "got" marketing. But it still took some persistence on my part, and there were many weeks where I'd have to get him into the room to record our podcast. But he trusted me, and I made it easy for him. We had a format that just required him to basically be interviewed by me, once a week, for thirty minutes. From there, we could build our relationship and develop a podcast that would connect with our intended audience.

This focus on building an audience in a niche (niche meaning we focused specifically on content for people who might buy from Drift; so mainly people in sales and marketing roles, since Drift sold sales and marketing software) meant that when we finally launched our product, we already had thousands of people who had heard about Drift. They had an affinity for the brand because they got to feel like they could know, like, and trust the founder before launching. That trust led to preorders and great early sales. That created a tremendous advantage for Drift, and we have continued to use this model as we have developed new products. And by the way, that was all by design. David Cancel and his co-founder, Elias Torres, hired me to do exactly this—build an audience well before the company was ready to sell its products. I joined Drift in October 2015, and we did not "launch" Drift until April 2016. While the engineers and designers in the company were building the product, David and I were focused on marketing the company and building an audience so that when we were ready to sell, we wouldn't have to do it cold. People would already have a connection to Drift. To put numbers to the model, by the time we were ready to launch our product, we had over *three thousand* people lined up on a waiting list for the Drift product. Instead of trying to scrape together a list of potential customers we could cold email, we had a list of thousands of people who already knew us and were ready to learn more. I'm pretty sure the first email we sent was something like: *"So we haven't tried to sell you anything in six months, but today we'd be silly if we didn't reach out to tell you about our new product and why we think you're going to love it."*

This process and its success changed my career. Prior to working for Drift, I was a junior-level marketing person. I was an average marketing manager making an average salary, trying to figure out what to do with my career. With the success of building the founder's brand at Drift, I was able to help Drift become one of the fastest growing SaaS companies of all time, growing past $30 million in annual recurring revenue in under two years, and along the ride I was able to grow my career from marketing manager to VP of Marketing managing a team of thirty people. After Drift, I joined Privy as Chief Marketing Officer, where I took a similar playbook of building a brand for the founder/CEO Ben Jabbawy. This led us to launch Ben's *E-commerce Marketing School* podcast, which was downloaded over 250,000 times. Privy became an established leader in their slice of the market, and eighteen months later the company sold to Attentive in a nine-figure deal.

If you have a founder who is willing to become the face of the brand, ready to be active on social media, and passionate about telling the company's story, building a "founder brand" can be an incredible way to build a business, especially if you're entering a crowded, competitive, or even brand-new market.

THE FOUNDER ADVANTAGE

Today, people want to buy from people. We want to work with people who we know, like, and trust. And this is why I believe that the clearest path to success in marketing (if your goal is to build awareness for your brand) is to start with the founder. A founder with a brand gives your marketing efforts superpowers. A founder brand builds trust, creates lasting relationships, and conveys expertise, leadership, content, and personality.

Let's look at the benefit each superpower brings to your marketing efforts:

- **Trust:** People want to buy from *people*, and we want to trust the brands we buy. When the founder and brand coincide, people feel they're buying from a person they can trust, not an anonymous brand—and that trust transfers to the brand or product. Founders give a sense of authority and believability.

- **Expertise:** The founder often has deep expertise/experience in an industry, and people want to be led by an expert. Whether I am going to the doctor, buying a car, building a house, getting personal training, or in need of sales training, I want to work with an expert. Customers are more skeptical than ever, and one way to cut through that skepticism is to lead with your expertise. The founder is often uniquely positioned to do this.

- **Leadership:** Every great movement has a leader. Clearly announcing who the leader is and what the leader does gives credibility to your brand. Steve Jobs was the leader of the "Think Different" movement for Apple, but even on a smaller scale, people want a leader. If you are a startup in the financial world, the opportunity is not just to offer a product, but to teach people a new way of thinking about finance for the future. And the best way to get that story to stick is to have it be told by a person, not a faceless brand. The founder should be the leader of your movement. The spokesperson. The person to know, like, trust, and follow.

- **Content:** Because the founder is an expert, they often have the most "internal knowledge" about the industry, the market, the competition, the landscape, the best practices, and the trends. David Cancel's knowledge of the needs in product marketing comes to mind. His unique experience after twenty years in the sales and marketing industry gave the Drift team an incredible advantage because the founders had deep experience in this industry. We used that to our advantage to create content that would resonate with our audience. I didn't have all the marketing experience in the world as a twenty-eight-year-old marketing manager, but I could lean on the founders who did, and my job was to help amplify those stories.

- **Personality:** The brands that attract and create superfans today are the ones that are real, authentic, and human. Founders often have some type of interesting personality trait, history, stories, and, of course, quirks. All of this can build an authentic brand. Use the founder's personality to your advantage. People want the real you, not that corporate, stuffy version.

- **Relationships:** Founders have the relationships with investors, advisors, partners, industry analysts, and influencers. All of that can be used to your advantage in marketing because it gives you an incredible perspective on what is happening in your industry. The way to become a leader in your industry is not to promote your product 24/7 but to add value to others (ideally your potential customers). Founders are in so many interesting conversations each week, and all of that can build a brand by doing your work in public. Share commentary on meetings you had, people you met with, trends you're seeing.

Use these relationships to your advantage as a content creator.

These superpowers speed up securing your spot in people's minds and in your marketplace. They give you name recognition, relationships, and, ultimately, consumer loyalty, because people know there is an actual person behind the brand. Not a logo. Not a nameless, faceless corporation, but a real person. I call this advantage you get from a founder with a brand the founder advantage.

Every business can benefit from having a founder with a brand, but this strategy is especially powerful for startups.

When you're starting out with your business, you need every advantage you can find, and building a brand for the founder can give you an incredible wedge.

Yet, several factors block even the most successful startups from leaning into the founder advantage:

1. The founder doesn't know where to start building their brand or who to hire to do it.
2. The founder wants to create a brand but doesn't have the time.

3. The marketing team doesn't want to put in the necessary effort because they can't justify the ROI (return on investment).

4. The marketing team wants to build the founder's brand but doesn't have the time, bandwidth, or knowledge to do it.

I've been there and heard all the objections, from the founder doesn't have enough time, to "we don't know how to measure this," to "we have too many competing priorities." Yet, I've seen this work too many times to accept those excuses. I had to develop my own framework that replicates positive results repeatedly.

THE FOUNDER'S STORY MATTERS

Social media is the most powerful brand-building tool ever created.

The old way of building a brand was to wait for the press to notice you or to hire a public relations agency. I am oversimplifying, but before social media, media outlets controlled the spread of information, and it was almost impossible for a brand to get any attention from the press without a ridiculous stunt or a ridiculous amount of money from venture capitalists. But today, the game has changed. Any brand (and any founder) can reach their dream customers directly online, thanks to social media. In this world, you don't need to wait for the press. You are your own press, or at the very least, your own publisher. You can build your own media outlet.

This is why a founder with a brand is one of the best marketing channels you can have today. And if you don't have it yet, you can build it (we'll get there later on in this book). This strategy works so well because people want to work with people, put a face with a name, and feel like they "know" the owner of the business. But it also works well because most founders (at least the ones I've met) seem to always have something interesting going on. It's the reason they started the company, or the *way* they started the company. The deep cause or personal story that led them to start this business. The industry knowledge, expertise, and network. All of those ingredients are GOLD from a marketer's perspective. But most companies just never use that story. The only thing they ever "market" is the product and its features and benefits.

David Cancel, CEO of Drift, explained it this way: "I think it is important to build a brand as a founder." He explains that when a founder develops a brand, that brand has equity and value. The founder associated with the brand gives it legitimacy because of the reputation, trust, and following the founder has built *personally*. Like a musician who is well known, any album is likely to sell more than that of an unknown artist because of the name recognition and the artist's reputation. When it comes to founders of businesses, the same is true. If a founder launches something, it is likely that their followers will pay attention to the launch, adding that superpower to the marketing efforts. The audience for the new product or service will also grow by word-of-mouth due to the sense of connection that is the nature of personal brands. But unlike well-known musicians, the founder of a business doesn't have to build an audience of millions of followers online for the results to be meaningful.

David Cancel also stressed that the reason the founder brand is such a powerful tool is that humans crave connections and relationships with other humans. This is true for all people. For generations.

As you build and grow a founder's brand, the benefits multiply. You are more likely to draw strong candidates for hiring. Building a founder brand will bring you more inbound leads. It will help you attract your dream customers, some of them even before you have a product to sell. It will garner outside interest from investors instead of you having to identify and woo them.

Being a founder with a brand can bring you opportunities to speak at industry events, conferences, podcasts, and meet-ups. You might get included more in industry news, roundups, articles, and videos. And all of that can work to drive customers to your virtual or physical door. Plus, having a direct relationship with your dream customers online can also provide feedback for you and your company in regard to messaging, so you know what resonates with your target audience or niche. You'll literally have your finger on the pulse of your industry—without having to hire an analyst firm or do third-party research. You know what your potential customers want because you're in the conversations with them every day, online.

Now, I know what you might be thinking. You don't want the spotlight. You don't care about followers. You aren't one of those founders who wants to be out there in front of the camera.

But building a founder brand is not about vanity metrics. It's about *results*.

You started this company because you wanted to transform something—an industry, a customer's life, or a business process. This is about building a brand to build an audience, which is a competitive advantage. This is about being able to target your efforts to the right audience, the niche, rather than wasting time, money, and effort in the weeds searching for the customers.

Marketing is hard enough on its own. You're competing with other well-funded companies. You're competing for people's attention. This is about creating an advantage. Building a founder brand puts the wind at your back.

FOR YOU, THE FOUNDER

This book is for you, the founder. I've seen the impact, and I want you to make marketing part of your job. And the best part is that it doesn't require some huge budget or bleeding edge creativity to know what to do or say. My bet is that you are interesting enough *already*. Heck, you're the one crazy enough to go build a business. No one starts a company because it's supposed to be fun. It's hard work. But you've already taken the leap. You're the founder. And that also means you have deep industry knowledge, expertise, passion, or even some college-dorm-room crazy founding story. All you have to do is now go tell that story. And thanks to tools like social media and podcasting, it's easier than ever to reach your customers directly and build an audience on your own.

The brands that are going to flourish in the future are the brands where everyone knows the names of the people who work there. As part of that, potential customers should know the *founder* because that is who started the company.

Most companies only tell the story of their *products*. Telling the story of the *founder*, or at least telling it along with the story of the product, makes a huge difference in whether the business succeeds. Time and again my research shows the difference between thriving and withering lies in whether the business used the advantage of the founder brand.

I want to help other businesses—whether already running or about to launch—embrace and harness the power of the founder advantage and build a founder brand. In this book I will teach you the framework for building a brand as a founder. Or *for* your founder, if you're in the marketing team.[1]

If you are ready to commit, I'll show you how to unlock the founder advantage and build a founder brand. Be forewarned:

- There is no "six-minute abs" in this framework. This will require commitment and consistency.
- You must have something interesting to say, an interesting product, solution, or story—or be willing to learn to talk about your product, solution, or story in an interesting manner. Not saying you must be first. Not saying you must be Tesla. But you must have something interesting to say to your audience.

---

1   While you may be a member of a marketing team and are about to build a founder brand in your company, for the purpose of this book, we are talking directly to the founder. The "you" is the founder.

- You must be ready to embrace marketing and want to go on the offense.
- You must be ready to harness the power of social media.

In this framework, you'll discover how to become a storyteller, a publisher, and then the master of the feedback loop. You'll learn the strategies to build your founder brand, how and why they work, and how you can assess the impact they will have on your business. You'll see that the secret to gaining traction in any industry is becoming the guide and expert in that niche.

Before you learn the framework, know that I wrote it as a step-by-step process. There are three levels of building a brand as a founder:

- Level 1: Master the art of storytelling. Develop and refine your story.
- Level 2: Become a publisher. Don't wait for people to tell your story. Get on the offensive and go out and tell it.
- Level 3: Master the feedback loop. What can you learn from your metrics? Which metrics matter?

Why do I list them as levels and not steps? Each one is more advanced in its applications than the previous level, and I recognize that not all founders are ready or willing to tackle the more challenging aspects of this framework. Having said that, even just mastering your story and storytelling will reap benefits for your brand.

But what if you already have a company? A brand? A product? Should you still keep reading? Absolutely, because you still can build your founder brand.

Ben Jabbawy, CEO of Privy, was just that kind of founder. When I joined Privy, they already had a marketing team and a product, but as Ben built his *founder brand* following the steps in this framework, Privy grew exponentially. Just like Ben and David Cancel, you too can develop and implement your founder brand and enjoy the commercial benefits.

It's time to start. It's time to learn how to be a storyteller, a publisher, and a master of feedback.

It's time to embrace the founder advantage and build your brand as a founder.

LEVEL

1

BECOME A STORYTELLER

n our conversations, Hiten Shah would ask me about my marketing plans for Drift. After I wandered a bit, he finally suggested forgetting about marketing *Drift* at that moment, as the product hadn't been developed yet, and instead focus on marketing *David Cancel*.

I was about to launch the first founder brand by starting with David's story.

When I started down that road, we didn't expect him to become a household name, but we did want to build trust with potential customers before we tried to sell them something. How did we take an unknown company without a product to the heights of success it has now? By building a brand around the founder, David Cancel. His founder brand began by him telling his interesting story to the world.

STORYTELLING

Humans have been telling stories for millennia. Before written language, they were told orally. Before that, through paintings. We know our ancestors were telling stories through cave paintings over 64,000 years ago.

Written stories appeared about 9,000 years ago and started with pictorial languages before evolving to letter-based writing as we know it today. Whether stories were told in pictures, orally, or in written alphabetic language, they all were intended to impart knowledge, share history, and, most times, share a moral or a common cultural understanding. Think back to stories that your parents or grandparents read to you as a child. Those stories were rich in pictures. They entertained you, and they taught you a shared value such as honesty.

Anthropologists feel human beings are the only species that, to our knowledge, tells stories. These stories carry great power because they educate and entertain and engage with our senses. For example, the story of "Little Red Riding Hood" gives us the vivid imagery of a young girl wearing her red cloak, while "The Little Red Hen" entices us with the description of the smell of the bread baking in her kitchen. They evoke emotions as humans build relationships with the characters, and when tragedies hit, readers or listeners mourn with the characters.

Stories create synaptic connections in our brains that both tie in with our emotions and also connect with our cognition.

Stories are passed down from generation to generation and spread throughout the world. Many of the most commonly recognized childhood fables even cross cultural and linguistic borders, such as the basic story of Cinderella appearing across the globe in a multitude of cultures. Stories may be factual, such as *The Diary of Anne Frank,* or they may be completely fictional, such as "Rumpelstiltskin." They all have the purpose of teaching, inspiring, or entertaining us.

The same is true of the stories used in the building of great brands. We know the stories of founders such as Steve Jobs and how he co-founded Apple. That particular story was so gripping and engaging, it led to books and movies. There are many others, such as Zoom founder Eric Yuan, Shopify founder Tobias Lütke, and Hint founder Kara Goldin. These founders weren't unusual in having a great story. Anyone launching a business has a reason for doing it, and there is a story that can be shared.

The importance of storytelling for a founder building a brand cannot be overstated. In our noisy, busy, technological world, humans are spending more time with screens than with humans, and a story is a way to connect with other people, albeit virtually, at a deep, almost primal, emotional level. It is the quickest and easiest way to build relationships with a large audience and to therefore have them feel empowered and connected to you and your brand.

The key to using storytelling in your brand is to know how to tell your story and target the delivery of the story to the correct audience, to the *niche* that wants the product or service your business provides. For example, Sara Blakely's story resonates with women, particularly professional women, and she focused her business's niche on that audience. If Sara had instead blanketed all of the airwaves with that story, many people for whom it had no possible personal significance would have tuned out. Sara targeted her niche with a great story, and you can do the same.

To see the power of a story and the connection it makes with a potential audience, go on YouTube and search for Steve Jobs's iPhone Keynote Address from 2007. In that example, as well as countless others, Steve Jobs showed that beyond everything else, he was a master of storytelling, and ultimately his role at Apple was to be the CSO, the Chief *Storytelling* Officer.

Follow the framework, and you too will be the Chief Storytelling Officer of your company.

HOW TO DEVELOP YOUR STORY

Every founder has a story that is interesting. That story provides engaging content and context long before talking about any products or specs, and it works. Almost always, the founding story makes for great marketing content.

Why does the founder's story matter? As Erik Jacobson, the founder of Lemonpie, one of the top podcast production agencies for B2B brands today like HubSpot, Buffer, ConvertKit, and ProfitWell, says, "The founder is the person that people will resonate with the most."

The first step is framing the founder's story. This is beyond an elevator pitch and more about thinking about the whole story as it relates to your product. The founder is the leader of this movement, but the story must tie back to the company. I've found answering these six questions to be a great framework for laying out the key ingredients in the company and founder story:

- What is the founder's (your) backstory?
- What's the problem your business exists to solve?
- Who's the villain your customers are facing?
- What's the solution that you offer?
- What are the benefits of using your product?
- What's life like before and after using your product?

Simple questions, right? By answering them, the founder's story becomes clear. For example, imagine a mother who was raising her kids, wanting to make sure they had the best nutrition. Day after day, the lack of healthy and tasty beverage options frustrated her. Sugary drinks were everywhere, but her kids weren't going to drink them. The solution was to develop her own line of healthy, yummy, kid-approved drinks that were easy to take anywhere. The benefits were clear: her kids were happy and healthy. Now, kids can be with their friends and have a great beverage option without destroying their health.

By answering those six questions, the founder's story comes to life.

Let's dig into those questions more. Let's think about exactly what information should be included in those answers, both to build the brand's credibility and also target the right niche.

Using Sara Blakely as an example, let's look at those questions again, and answer them:

- *What is the founder's backstory?* Sara was a successful business owner.
- *What's the problem?* Sara was getting ready to go to a party, wanting to wear a pair of white pants, and

didn't have the right undergarment to wear with them. Anything she had would show color-wise or give her panty lines.

- *Who's the villain?* Undergarments that didn't work for the current fashions.

- *What's the solution?* By cutting off the legs of a pair of pantyhose, she instantly created the perfect solution for what to wear under that pair of slacks. She then went on to found a multimillion dollar company selling such undergarments.

- *What are the benefits?* Women can look sleek in their clothes and be comfortable at the same time.

- *What's life like before and after?* Women are more self-confident and feel more attractive wearing Spanx. As they are comfortable too, it is a win-win situation.

Using Drift as an example:

- *What is the founder's backstory?* David (Drift CEO) had spent the last ten years building sales and marketing software (credibility, authority, trust, proof).

- *What's the problem?* The traditional way of doing sales and marketing is broken. It has made buying too challenging for potential customers (takes too long to get in touch with a company, many hoops to jump through in order to buy, frustrating customer experience).
- *Who's the villain?* Lead forms. The sales and marketing tools most companies are forced to use are built for the old world, not how people buy today. So we made lead forms the villain. Not a specific competitor. But we made the villain a shared enemy: lead forms. Something that everyone can relate to. No one wants to fill out lead forms, so we made lead forms the villain in our story.

Now do it for yourself as a founder. Answer these questions, digging deeper into your own backstory.

- What is the founder's backstory? You don't need to include every bit of your story, only the parts that connect in some way with your product.

What were you doing just prior to the idea that sparked your business idea? Be honest and be vulnerable. For example:

- **Shopify Founder Tobi Lütke:** In 2004, Lütke, along with his partners, Daniel Weinand and Scott Lake, launched Snowdevil, an online snowboard shop. Lütke built a new e-commerce platform for the site, using Ruby on Rails because they couldn't find an existing tool that made it easy for them to build their own online store. Soon after, the Snowdevil founders shifted their focus from snowboards to e-commerce and launched Shopify in 2006. Shopify was built to solve this initial problem.[2]

- **Zoom Founder Eric Yuan:** Yuan joined Webex, a web conferencing startup, where he was one of the first twenty hires. The company was acquired by Cisco Systems in 2007, at which time Yuan became vice

---

2   "Tobias Lütke," Wikipedia.org, November, 2021, https://en.wikipedia. org/wiki/Tobias_L%C3%BCtke.

president of engineering. In 2011, Yuan pitched a new smartphone-friendly video conferencing system to Cisco management. When the idea was rejected, Yuan left Cisco to establish his own company, Zoom Video Communications.[3]

- **Calendly Founder Tope Awotona:** Awotona would spend a day wasting a lot of time going back and forth over email to schedule meetings. So he started searching for a scheduling tool, but all the products he found were slow and clunky. After months of research, he went all in with this idea. He put every single dollar he had made into this new business.

- **Hint Founder Kara Goldin:** After having three children, Goldin realized she wanted to spend her time creating and living a healthy lifestyle. She had trouble losing the additional

---

3   "Eric Yuan, Wikipedia.org, November, 2021, https://en.wikipedia.org/wiki/Eric_Yuan.

baby weight and came upon the realization that everything she was drinking was sugary, unhealthy, and artificially sweetened. Goldin then took this idea and launched Hint in 2005 in San Francisco.[4]

- What's the problem? Is it a product that doesn't exist, and you had to invent it? A service that you needed and couldn't find? A way to solve a common problem or concern?

- Who's the villain? Or what? Why is this a problem? Why would someone want to rid themselves of this villain?

- What's the solution? Plain and simple, how do you solve this problem? What product or service are you specifically proposing to provide, and how does it solve the problem?

---

4   "Kate Goldin," Wikipedia.org, November, 2021, https://en.wikipedia.org/wiki/Kara_Goldin.

- What are the benefits? State the clear and compelling benefits of using your product. How do you make your customers' lives better? Don't focus on features but focus on the selfish benefits people will get by using your product. How do you help them make money? Save money? Save time? Increase status? Improve health?

- What's life like before and after? One of the best things you can do in your marketing and storytelling is to actually *show* your customers what life is like before and after using your product. So do it. Get in the weeds and be specific. Spell out what will be different in their life before and after using your product. As my friend Ryan Deiss (CEO of DigitalMarketer) has schooled me many times on the whiteboard: In the "Before" state, the customer is discontent in some way. They might be in pain, bored, frightened, or unhappy for any number of reasons. In the "After" state, life is better. They are free of pain, entertained, or unafraid of what previously plagued them. You need to map these out for your product and your story. What is life like before and after your product?

The more transparent, open, and potentially emotionally vulnerable you are in your story, the easier it is for your niche to feel a connection. For example, when Richard Branson talks about how much he hated school because it was so difficult for him and he often felt stupid, every former student who walked home from school feeling intellectually inferior identifies with him. They listen more closely to his words, watch his actions, and, ultimately, buy whatever he is selling. And it's one of the reasons I love social media for founder brand building: people want to work with you. The real you. Not the corporate you. Not the nameless, faceless company. So you need to actually put *yourself* in the story.

Some founders will chafe at the idea of having to answer those exact six questions. After all, having started a company, telling your story is easy, right? Having worked with many founders over the years, I have realized that a formulaic approach to building the story leads to far better results. The stories are more complete and relatable, and they have a more profound impact on the listeners.

This is not the time to go rogue. Just answer the questions. And even though some of them might seem obvious, it's the exercise of sitting down and mapping out answers to each one of these ingredients and then weaving them all together to develop your story. These are the time-tested principles. Now it's up to you whether you're going to put them into play or not.

CHAPTER 2

FIND YOUR NICHE AND DEFINE YOUR ENEMY

n order to get your story to cut through the noise and attract your dream customers, you will need to do two key things: the first is to focus on a specific niche, and the second is to define your enemy. I'll explain them both in this section.

BEGIN WITH A NICHE

Let's start with the definition of niche. A niche is a specialized segment of the market for a particular kind of product

But I prefer the other way to say it: the riches are in the niches.

When you have a niche, it means that you have a clear focus on your intended, targeted customer for *today*. You need to be specific about your intended audience *right now*. If you are struggling to get traction (or just starting out, which is why you might be reading this book now), it will do you no good to focus on the masses because you will be lost in the noise. Creating a niche allows you to re-segment the market and speak to individual customers. From there, you have a foundation on which to build. I know you might have big, billion-dollar, household-brand-name goals, but "niching" down is one of the greatest marketing strategies you can develop to get initial traction. One of my favorite quotes about marketing comes from Roy H. Williams in *The Wizard of Ads*: "The risk of insult is the price of clarity." If you try to appeal to everyone, you will often appeal to no one. It's just as important to understand who you are not focusing on and being explicit about those audiences in your marketing.

Let me give you an example from Drift. At the time of Drift's inception, there were more than 5,000 other sales and marketing tools similar to Drift already in the market (well over 10,000 today). If we had pitched to a larger niche group, we would have joined *five thousand* of our competitors, all scratching and clawing for a tiny piece of the marketing pie. Despite the company's billion-dollar ambitions and selling to 3-4-5 different personas and types of customers, we made a conscious decision to start by focusing on one buyer: one tiny slice and subsection of marketers—product marketers. I do not know the audience size, but I bet that "product marketers" are less than 10 percent of Drift's total addressable market. Why did we narrow a potential audience of marketers down to just *product* marketers? We needed a wedge, a way into the market.

We didn't have any traction yet; marketing to the masses and trying to sell to all of those personas would have been a costly mistake. Instead, we niched down and focused specifically on one slice of the market. And our plan was to use *those* learnings to figure out how to market and sell to other types of customers. If you don't mind me going back to my restaurant industry example for a minute: we bet that *if* people came to us for our cheeseburgers, we'd (over time) be able to also sell them our chicken sandwiches, cheesesteaks, and more.

We focused our marketing efforts not on sales or lead generation, but simply on becoming the trusted expert and authority on product marketing. Rather than trying to sell anyone anything, we focused on content and building up Drift as a great resource for product-marketing people to learn about product marketing. We focused only on the selfish benefit of our potential customers: *"Help me get smarter at my job. If I get smarter at my job, I'll find more success at work; I'll get promoted. If I get promoted, I can put a down payment on a house..."*

So we created a newsletter focused specifically on product marketers. It started as a curated weekly recap of links. I was a product marketer myself in a previous life, so I had a sense of whom to follow on Twitter, what blogs to read, and how to get a sense for what the "industry" was talking about. Each week, we'd send out an email with some of the best product marketing content we'd found that week. That email list grew, because the content was genuinely helpful and there was never a Drift sales pitch or even mention of our product. *And that's not because I didn't want to! It's because we didn't have anything to sell them yet. We were still close to six months away from launching our product*. Plus, the newsletter had another nice thing about it: product marketers wanted to send us their own articles and ideas, because they wanted to get featured in our newsletter. Next, we built a blog with the same focus. We took the email content and expanded on it. And because we already had the newsletter, we already had a sense of the type of content people were interested in. Over time, we started creating our *own* content and commentary on product marketing. We did interviews with product marketers. We published templates and decks and helpful resources. Then in our weekly product marketing newsletter, we started sending people back to *our* site with our *own* content (vs. always sharing other people's stuff), and that combination led us to build an audience of product marketers, and that became our very clear niche.

This strategy can be applied to almost any industry and any business. And the result for Drift was that well before we launched, we already had an audience. We had built awareness for Drift in a niche with our dream customers (product marketers) before we even had anything to sell them.

Many startups struggle to choose one niche. There will be trade-offs: Yes, there are some segments or markets you could focus on and also do well. Yes, you might say no to an area where you could also be successful. But the time and effort it takes to determine and target your niche will pay you back handsomely as you build an audience. As you build an audience in one area, you can easily use those learnings to move into the next niche (and you'll already have an audience and have learned some lessons about what works/doesn't, and you can apply that to the next niche or market segment to be even more successful).

For example, you are a woman who wants to develop a new fitness program/brand. Will you be the first? No. By finding your niche, you can still be very successful with your brand. Can you be the first woman-owned fitness brand in Burlington, Vermont, that caters to working moms who want to bring their children to the gym for art/music classes while they work out? Could you also be the first brand to offer to-go meals you could order and take home when you are done working out? Yes, that would be a niche. The niche would be working moms who want an enrichment activity for their children and a healthy meal to take home after working out. That level of specificity is a *niche*.

Fast-forward several years in Drift's history, and today the company has—as planned—evolved well beyond product marketing. Drift serves the entire sales and marketing function inside of a company. That is a vast market. But momentum and progress into that market all started because we decided early on to focus on a niche. That niche became our wedge. Once we learned how to talk to product marketers, we used the knowledge from those marketing efforts to market Drift to demand generation teams, and then field marketing, and then inside sales, and then outside sales, and now *all* of those teams combined. It all starts like this: define a niche, build an audience of people in that niche through your content (which gets people to know, like, and trust you well before they are ready to buy from you), listen and learn from that audience, and then design products and services that match those people's needs.

During my tenure as Chief Marketing Officer, Privy was focusing their marketing solution on e-commerce, but that was too broad. There are literally hundreds of millions of e-commerce stores, selling products that range from $1 to $1 million, and three to five customer segments

Privy could have gone after. Instead, Privy's Founder and CEO Ben Jabbawy played to his strengths and focused on a niche: *small* e-commerce brands. Ben has small business roots through his family, so he had a natural connection to the space. He also used his experience to create an advantage: as someone close to the small business space, Ben realized that while there were many brands that said they served small businesses, few actually provided small business owners with the three key ingredients they needed to succeed: a product that is super easy to use, education on how to build a better business, and one-on-one service and support (being able to actually talk to a real human). So at Privy, we niched our marketing efforts to focus on small e-commerce brands. And to get everyone on the same page internally and externally, we even defined what small means: a business that is doing less than one million dollars in sales per year and who doesn't have a ton of resources or a full marketing team. This is how you focus on a niche. And if you're reading along at home right now, I hope you're nodding along.

To give you one more well-known example of using a niche, consider Tesla. In 2008, Tesla focused on their niche of one (their first) electric car, making just one model. Today, if you look at their website, it says, "Tesla is accelerating the world's transition to sustainable energy with electric cars, solar and integrated renewable energy solutions for homes and businesses." Starting with that small niche in 2008, they have grown exponentially since then. They started with one model of a car, learned, iterated, and then kept scaling. You can do this at any level of business and with any product. For example: I could use this book as the wedge to create multiple other books in the future, but I'm starting with this niche to learn.

HOW DO I PICK MY NICHE?

The best way to pick a niche is to work backward. Based on what you can offer *today*, who is your ideal customer? *Today* is the keyword; think about your present ideal customer, not one based on the features and benefits and future products you might be building. I want you to be honest with yourself. As of right now, who is a good fit to buy your product? (By the way, if the answer is no one, it's time to go back to the drawing board and develop some type of product roadmap; but this is a marketing book, so I expect that you're here with some type of product offering already.)

Drift's chatbot product needed to be installed on a company's website, and inside of the typical companies Drift was selling to, the website was either (a) controlled by product marketing, or (b) influenced by product marketing. So we focused on product marketing because we thought that product marketing could be our *wedge* into getting Drift installed on a company website. We knew that if we couldn't get Drift installed on the website, we wouldn't have a business. We bet on product marketing, and we focused our marketing strategy there.

Another way to think about picking a niche is to think about what your minimum addressable market is. In the Drift example, we even started off smaller than product marketers: we initially focused on product marketers in Boston, since that's where we were based and had connections. Then we took that knowledge from in-person discussions with product marketers in Boston to reach product marketers everywhere through our content, social media, and podcasts.

Marketing is a game of momentum. Similar to the NBA sharpshooter who needs to make a few layups to get loose, you need to build momentum with your marketing. Start with a niche, build an audience in that niche, learn, and then expand.

What if the niche is too small? This is one question I usually hear when talking about this topic, and here's what I say: I've rarely found this to be the case. The good news is that you'll learn quickly if your niche is too small. Too small means there will either be no customers in that segment, or not *enough* customers in that segment (you'll have to use the economics of your business to define that one). But in either case, if you've learned the niche you're targeting is too small, that is already a victory! You can rule out that option and target something bigger until you find a wedge that works.

A few parting words for you to chew on as you think about defining your niche. Study the laws of marketing Two of my favorite marketing lessons come from Al Ries and Jack Trout's book, *The 22 Immutable Laws of Marketing*. The first law is the Law of Leadership, which states it's better to be first than it is to be better. "The basic issue in marketing is creating a category you can be first in. It's the law of leadership: it's better to be first than it is to better. It's much easier to get into the mind first than to try to convince someone you have a better product than the one that did get there first." If you can do it, be first. Getting into the mind first is valuable real estate. "The leading brand in any category is almost always the first brand in the prospect's mind." But be careful. Find the right line here between being first and being a gimmick. If the first is a genuine claim that benefits customers meaningfully, use it to your advantage.

The second *Immutable Law* is also worth noting here: The Law of the Category. If you can't be first in an existing category, set up a new category you can be first in. And yes, the gimmick rule from above applies here too. There is no category of blue water bottles or cars that have an extra cup holder ☺.

THE VILLAIN IN YOUR STORY

It's Saturday night, and you are cuddled up on the couch with your significant other, watching a movie—for example,

Remember the Titans—and the villain is making your blood boil. In that case, the villain is systemic racism.

All great movies, books, and stories have a villain or an enemy. Sometimes, the villain is a single person, such as Cruella de Vil in 101 *Dalmatians*. Sometimes it is a disease, a company, or a team. The status quo is often the villain, as humans strive to improve that which already exists.

Why does it matter in this process? Can't you have a great business brand without a villain? You can, but you decided to read this book, so I'm going to give you the secret: you create an advantage in marketing when you create a villain. A villain allows you to tap into the art of storytelling, gives you a conflict, and allows for conflict resolution. You want your brand's product or service to be seen as the resolution to that struggle. You are here to save the day. Your brand exists to free your customer from this struggle. To relieve their pain. To solve their biggest problem and tackle that hairy challenge they haven't been able to solve without you.

Going back to Drift, our villains were those dreaded lead forms you needed to complete to get a simple answer to a question. *Everyone* hates those forms. My mother-in-law hates them, and when we focused on that particular villain at Drift, it was a message she could understand and embrace. Even if she didn't understand exactly what Drift was doing, she definitely understood how much she disliked those forms, and she rooted for a product that would slay them.

A villain serves a clear purpose in a founder brand. It shows why you should go with this particular company. It shows your potential customers that you understand their pain, and you want to help them, thus helping form a relationship with them. How did we use Drift's villain tactically? We interwove the villain through every aspect of our business communications and marketing. For example:

- We created content, such as articles, videos, and podcasts, that were rallying our supporters and educating followers about what we were doing to solve the lead form problem.
- We created the "No Forms" movement and did things such as make stickers we'd send out to customers, give away at events, and use in our social media posts.

- We created the category of Conversational Marketing—strategic positioning for the company—creating a whole new industry.
- We wrote a book about the evils of lead forms and how we had solved the problem.
- When we were ready to launch our product, we held a big coming-out party, and we announced we were signaling the end of lead forms, and it resonated with our followers and caused such enthusiasm that it translated to paying customers.

Those lead forms gave us a villain that most people in product marketing could hate *with* us, and it created a sense of community and a group of potential customers for Drift.

A few lessons on your villain. First, if you are identifying a villain, make sure you aren't also using that villain in some way. For example, if you started a brand based upon the idea of a healthy alternative to soda for children, it will derail your credibility if every picture you post on your founder's Instagram account has your children drinking sodas. You can't fake this. It has to be a real, authentic part of your brand and story. This almost bit us at Drift, as we were declaring to our niche that we had an alternative to lead forms, but, gasp, we were still using lead forms on Drift's website. So instead, we turned this into an opportunity and made a public declaration that we would not use lead forms anymore and that we were going to document this new way of doing marketing on our blog, in our emails, and on our podcast to show people how they could do the same. I love the idea of "working in public" as a brand, sharing what you're doing as you're doing it. That works really well here since most people will be skeptical. Even though they agree with your villain, they often haven't seen the solution yet. So we turned what could have been a credibility disaster into one of our best marketing channels: we told the story of how we were building Drift without lead forms as we were doing it. This was a perfect fit with our audience of marketers. But for you, this might be something else: if you're a sales coach with a new way of doing sales, prove it. Show your secret sauce. Do your work in public. Show how you're attacking this villain by actually *proving* it. Show your work. Show the results. There can be no misdirection in marketing anymore. Proof and results win, so if you have a better way of doing things, show it. Document it: it's the best content for social media.

The other thing to remember with your villain is that your villain must be *obvious*. When you talk about your villain, everyone in your niche should nod along like, "Yes! I have this problem too!"

Just like we talked about with your niche/category in the last section, your villain can't be a marketing gimmick—it must be real. For example, at Privy, selling to small e-commerce businesses, the villain was *complexity*. Most small business owners found it too hard, too confusing, or too time consuming to do marketing. At Privy, our mission was to be the brand that helped you conquer that villain. The result was effective marketing that allowed customers to build profitable e-commerce businesses without having to hire an agency, be an expert in marketing, or have technical website experience.

YOUR TURN

Now you need to determine your niche and your villain. In order to do so, you need to answer the following questions:

- What is the market I want to enter?

- Who is the target customer? Be as specific as possible. Don't say "women," say, "women, twenty-five to thirty, college educated, living in the suburbs, not married, no children." You want a group small enough that you can get their attention, but big enough that they can reach out to others.

- The best way to pick a niche is to work backward. Based on what you can offer today, who is your ideal customer? Not based on the features and benefits and future products you might be building. I want you to be honest with yourself. As of right now, who is a good fit to buy your product?

- What problem are you trying to solve and why? Be specific.

Brainstorm your ideas. A list is a great place to start. Then, start clarifying your answers. It's not enough to say, "The problem was a lack of healthy beverages that taste good to kids." It's time to clarify your answers, for example, "The juice boxes and bottled beverages marketed for young children were high in corn syrup and also had added flavors and preservatives."

As we move into developing your explainer, we will take your answers and boil them down so you can immediately and consistently have a conversation with anyone in your niche about exactly what you can do to improve their lives.

CHAPTER 3

NOW YOU NEED AN EXPLAINER

Now that you have clarified your niche and answered your six questions that will shape your story and determined your villain, it is time to turn it into something you can use. Here you are going to boil down all of that detail and information into a short, memorable statement, an explainer, that can be used in actual conversations—not just sit in a PDF document somewhere inside of your company.

This is where many traditional positioning and messaging frameworks miss the mark. They don't give you something you can use in a regular conversation. Conversations are where you will generate connections and ultimately sales. Think about all of those meetings with potential investors or current investors, industry events, or interviews and podcasts. If you don't have something you can easily and consistently use in those conversations, your brand is belly-up, dying in the water already.

THE EXPLAINER

The goal of the explainer is to get the *attention* of your potential audience (audience could mean your dream customers, investors, partners, and future employees). Once you have their attention, you can tell them everything they need to know about your products and services.

This is where my favorite copywriting lesson comes into play. That lesson is "first line, second line." The goal of the first line of your copy should always be to get someone to read your second line of copy. The goal of the second line of copy should be to get them to read the third. All the way until they have finished reading. This is a technique I rely on to write compelling copy, and you can use it to create your explainer too.

When I write an explainer, they are two to three sentences long. The perfect length for a short conversation. The format is like this:

1. You know how _____ (insert the problem or old way of doing things that you aim to change)?
2. Instead of _____ (problem/old way), we have a _____ (solution/new way).
3. We call it _____ (name of the product or brand).

That is a brief conversation that can become your explainer. I like this format because it allows you to explain in a natural way what your company does. I've been inside of companies where the employees say—as if on autopilot—whatever corporate jargon message the PR team gave them to memorize and repeat and that never works. Instead, I suggest explaining the company like I would to a friend in conversations: "you know how...well, instead of... we call it..."

Drift's Explainer

In the corporate PR example I mentioned above, here's how this likely plays out. Let's say I'm at an event and a potential customer comes up to me and says, "Hey, what does Drift do exactly?"

I might say: "We are the leading conversational marketing platform." And she will probably say "interesting" or "huh" or nothing at all. And right there, the conversation is over before it started.

Using the model above, the conversation is very different.

The potential customer says, "Hey, what does Drift do exactly?"

I grin, because not only do I know the answer, I know how to *explain* it to her. "You know sometimes when you go to someone's website you have to fill out ten forms just to get a question answered?"

She smiles and nods. "Yeah. I hate that."

Now I've hooked her. We're actually going to have a conversation! She's going to get this!

"Instead of making people jump through hoops and all those lead forms," I continue on, "Drift is like having a

24/7 virtual assistant live on your website to help your customers buy."

Her eyes widen. "Interesting. How do you do that?" And she means it. She *is* interested in the answer. The key part here is *how do you do that*. If you have built a company or product that solves a real problem that a target customer is having, this is how they will respond: "Interesting. How do you do that?" This is an invitation to *tell her more*. Now, this does not guarantee that Drift can cure every pain and solve the problems that she's having, but I'm at least heading down that road.

Now I can I say, "Well, we call it Conversational Marketing," and then I can explain what we do in detail. I can talk about the product and how it works and the features and benefits. I can name-drop customers and give examples. I've painted a picture she can understand and relate to by using "you know how...well, instead of... we call it..." to start a conversation instead of a dead-end, glazed eyes response. Then this explainer can guide everything you create as a brand, from your homepage headline, email signatures, ad copy, and anywhere else in your marketing.

Examples from Other Brands

Here's an example from Gong. Gong calls what they do Revenue Intelligence. If you just heard "revenue intelligence," would you know what that means? I don't think most people would.

On their website, they explain it in a conversational way. They say, "[You can] gain critical insights into what's happening with your remote sales team, your deals, and your market with Revenue Intelligence from Gong."

Using my framework for an explainer, I would put it, "You know how hard it is to track all of your sales activity in one place? Well, we help you see what's happening with your remote sales team, your deals, and your market. We call it Revenue Intelligence." *That* explains what Gong does in a way that catches the attention of the listener.

Here's an example from Shopify. Most people know that they are an e-commerce platform, but on their website they lead with "Anyone, anywhere, can start a business."

What does that tagline really tell you? Instead, envision it using my framework.

I say to a new acquaintance, "You know how it's really hard to sell stuff online? Well we've (Shopify) created a platform that makes it easy for anyone, anywhere to build an online business."

The natural next question for anyone interested in Shopify at this point is to say "Interesting. How?"

This framework puts you in a position where your target customers are asking you questions, and that's where you want to be. You don't have to explain every spec and every feature in the first two minutes of a conversation. You want to provide context to maintain their curiosity so they say, "Interesting. How?" This framework also *allows* you to use the tagline (i.e., Conversational Marketing, Revenue Intelligence) without sounding like jargon or a buzzword, because you've actually explained what the heck it means.

YOUR TURN

Step 1: Having seen the examples above, it's time for you to develop your own explainer for your brand. Here is the format again:

1. You know how _____(insert the problem or old way of doing things that you aim to change)?

2.   Instead of _____(problem/old way), we have a _____(solution/ new way).

3.   We call it _____(name of the product or brand or category you've created).

Try it. Write it out, share it with people who *do* understand what your brand does, and then try it on someone who has no clue what the company does. See their reactions. It should be a conversation starter, and if it isn't, it's time to edit and revamp the explainer.

So far I've given you some simple frameworks to help define your niche, develop your story, create a villain, and nail down a company explainer. Now you need some role models, mentors, and anti-role models from whom you can learn on a daily basis. They teach us who we want to become and what we want to avoid, and they help us envision our own success. The beginning sections of this book are all about making sure you have the right ingredients. We need to make sure you're set up for success to build a founder brand; and then later we'll talk more about how to actually go and do it with the help of social media and podcasting.

CHAPTER 4

FIND YOUR ROLE MODELS, MENTORS, AND ANTI-ROLE MODELS

A ustin Kleon wrote that every artist is asked the question, "Where do you get your ideas?" The honest artist answers, "I steal them." Picasso said it. Steve Jobs said it. Austin Kleon references it in his brilliant book on creativity *Steal Like an Artist*.

Stealing, however, is not about blindly copying. It is about figuring out what is worth stealing and why, and then developing your own version of it as it applies to you and your business in the context in which you are operating. There is very little in the world that is completely original, and history has a way of repeating itself. You want to consider three types of personal models as you build your founder brand:

- Role Model: someone you look up to professionally, who has achieved what you want to achieve.
- Mentor: someone in a similar industry (or the same industry) but who is a step or two ahead of you.
- Anti-Role Model: the person you learn about to make sure you don't replicate their process by accident.

ROLE MODELS

The goal of finding a role model is to find a comparable company that has risen to the level of success to which you aspire. It's easier than ever today to unpack success from founders in your industry—you just have to make it a priority and become obsessed with studying their playbooks. Become a student of their marketing. Understand how they tell their story. Learn from them so you can adapt those models to your own business.

Ideally, this is someone in your industry. For example, if you are the founder of an e-commerce apparel company in the fitness space and want to build globally, Gymshark Founder and CEO Ben Francis would be a superb role model. You don't need to meet him. You don't need to pick his brain in person. Instead, find early Gymshark content on YouTube and search for his name on Spotify and Apple Podcasts. Listen to interviews he's given. Read things he's published. Find old tweets and articles. It's all out there somewhere. Narrow your choices to one or two role model founders and get obsessed with studying them and how they got to where they are (the same can be applied to companies too; if you want to be the next Salesforce, study everything they've done).

This advice sounds obvious, but it's missed by so many because it's easier to follow the masses and just read broader industry news. I want you to identify a founder as your role model and follow their every move. I did this personally a few years back. I wanted to boost my knowledge in marketing, specifically direct response marketing. ClickFunnels CEO Russell Brunson built a reputation as the best direct response marketer in the world, and he had been putting out a daily podcast for five years. I went back and listened to every single podcast episode. For months, that was the only podcast I listened to, and the lessons were incredible. I got what felt like firsthand experience listening to an amazing marketer build his business (his podcast was basically him sharing daily lessons about what he was doing as he was doing it). He would share new marketing experiments, campaign ideas, channels that worked/didn't work, and lessons from mentors and meetings he was in. I felt like I was drinking from the fire hose, because he was sharing almost daily marketing lessons as they were happening. He had already seen it all, and now I could get that wisdom indirectly. It was one of the best ways to speed up my learning: learning from someone who was doing something similar. Russell is one of the best audience builders I've seen in marketing, and I got his lessons directly as I was starting to learn and grow in my career in marketing. And then I got to digest those lessons and try to take the principles and use them for my projects.

Think about your niche. As you're reading this, you're probably nodding, thinking about who that might be in your industry. Following them on Twitter isn't enough—I want you to follow their every move. Listen to every interview. Read everything they write or that's written about them.

From role models, you learn what has worked for them, the idea being you'll avoid making the same mistakes they did. Learning from them will also allow you to achieve your goals more quickly, because you know the pitfalls to avoid. And even if you can't find a specific individual, you can find and follow broader trends. For example, when I was at Drift, I hadn't organized any big events, so I looked at events that companies similar to Drift had thrown, and I looked for what had been successful and what had been a mistake.

To use another example, if you are a parent, you have watched your child learn to walk. How do they learn? By watching you and other people do it for themselves. The toddler mimics what they see, as you are the role model. You should note that sometimes, your role model may not be a specific person; it may instead be a company, especially if the founder did not really publicize their process.

MENTORS

While you watch a role model from a distance, you have a personal relationship with a mentor.

Unlike a role model, this should be someone you can actually meet with regularly. And this is someone who should be in a similar industry (or the exact same industry) but who is a step or two ahead of you. You want to find direct access to someone who has already done what you're trying to do. For example, while I was running marketing at Drift, Mike Volpe was my mentor. Mike had spent the previous decade turning HubSpot (a high growth venture-backed SaaS company like Drift) from a startup into a billion-dollar, publicly traded unicorn. Mike had gone through everything I was trying to do (and if he hadn't, he had enough of the right first principles and decision-making frameworks to help).

As another example, Hiten Shah served as my mentor when he suggested I focus Drift's marketing effort on building a founder brand for David Cancel. Many times in that process, I reached out to bounce ideas off of Hiten to see what he thought. I trusted his advice and guidance, and I still do.

ANTI-ROLE MODELS

Paradoxical as it seems, the anti-role model provides guidance as much as the role model does. You learn what *not* to do.

For example, we all have heard of Facebook, but fewer and fewer people now remember Myspace (I will never forget Myspace, for what it's worth; my top eight friends will live on forever). Myspace had a brilliant marketing plan, appealing to young teens, but their technology struggled, and ultimately they couldn't compete against Facebook.

Charlie Munger is famous for his inversion framework. "Invert, always invert: Turn a situation or problem upside down. Look at it backward. What happens if all our plans go wrong?" I like to do the same with brand building. You must also identify who you do not want to be and study them. Especially in today's world, with so much access to information, you can learn about many mistakes before having to go through the pain of making them yourself.

CONNECTING WITH ROLE MODELS AND MENTORS

As a founder who is trying to build a brand (which is why you're here reading this book), there is no better shortcut than finding role models and mentors. When you think about the brand you want to build, who's already done it in your industry? And who's done it in a way that you like and admire? *That* is the person you should follow as you build your brand.

The connection with this role model may be completely aspirational, although the best role models typically will be founders in your industry. If possible, look for opportunities to connect with that person in real time and ideally in person. Are they speaking at a conference? Go to that event. Do you have a common connection? See if you can get an introduction.

Let's try a little exercise just to give you another example. I'll use this book and myself as an example here:

- Role Model(s): Gary Vaynerchuk, Ryan Holiday. Two successful entrepreneurs and authors who have had success with books about marketing like this one and often teach and speak about marketing. I've been following them online for years, reading their blogs, listening to their podcasts, and watching their moves. I don't have to meet them to have them as role models.

- Mentor: April Dunford. April is a marketing consultant and author of a brilliant book, *Obviously Awesome*. She would be a great person to work with as a mentor. She's been a guest on my podcast, so there's at least some chance of getting in touch with her. She would know all the pitfalls of writing and publishing a book in this niche.

- Anti-Role Model: There's one business book publishing company that is known for putting out books for companies, and they all read like jargony, corporate-stuffed crap. I want my book to feel modern, easy to understand, and tactical—I want people bookmarking, highlighting, and dog-earring this book. I don't want this book to be shelfware like one of those books would be.

WHY DO I NEED THEM?

Role models teach us how to do anything well, and they save us from reinventing the wheel. It is highly unlikely that you are the absolute first person to enter an industry or to target a particular niche. Therefore, knowing that you are not likely the first founder looking to drive down this road, finding role models helps you avoid the speed traps and potholes. Look for clues about where they found success and where they faltered. History is the greatest teacher.

For example, imagine that you are starting a new messaging platform. Your idea is unique because it solves a particular problem that exists on other platforms, but you still can learn from those who came before. Specifically, if you are looking at starting a messaging platform, you would want to look at the founders of Slack and WhatsApp. Read about them. Follow them on social media. See how they are mentioned in the press. Hear them speak in person or via podcast. Look to see where they succeeded and where they faltered. How did they get funding? Who did they connect with early in the process? How do they use social media now to grow their businesses? How have they pivoted and upscaled over the years? How did they use their own story, a niche, and the villain to move their brand forward?

Keep in mind, your role model in building your founder brand should be someone connected to what you aim to do. You will always have other role models, but they may not serve that same purpose in this process. For example, Nelson Mandela's consistent drive to end apartheid may make him someone you admire, but for this book and building your founder brand, he is not your role model. Your role model is the founder in your niche who has built a successful brand and an audience online with it.

Many great founders or entrepreneurs talk about how they needed to find role models to clarify their vision of themselves in their futures. They needed to learn from the role models everything from how to explain their passions to how to dress or act in public. Without a vision of what or who you are aspiring to be, it is hard to find your roadmap to success.

YOUR TURN

Brainstorm a list of at least five people who are potential role models (unless you already know the one perfect role model, then go with them), and look for ways in which you can learn from them.

As you make your list, think about *why* that person is a role model for you. Is it what they do professionally or how they achieved that success? Is it how they have broken down stereotypes or barriers? Is it because they are a leader in your industry? You may choose to have a company as a role model, to model your entire company after theirs.

With your list of names and ways to learn and connect with them, set a written plan for that learning. Make a commitment to that learning, whether it is listening to their audiobooks while you work out or podcasts while you cook dinner. If there are movies about the role models, schedule times to watch them. Don't wait for free time to do this learning. Schedule it into your days and evenings.

Make a list of potential mentors. Is there a professional organization where you can connect with others in your industry? Look through their membership listings to identify potential mentors and make a plan to reach out to them.

Finally, make a list of several anti-role models. Learn about them and reflect on why you *don't* want to emulate their process or them as people.

Once you have your list and have learned from them, it's time to put together the pieces and become a publisher of your story in order to fully embrace the power of the founder brand.

LEVEL

2

CHAPTER 5

BECOME A PUBLISHER AND GET ON SOCIAL MEDIA

The power of social media can be boiled down to the concept that as a founder, as anyone on social media, you now are your own publisher. You can control what, when, where, and why you publish. This becomes powerful when you focus on a niche and have a powerful story as presented earlier in this book. But instead of just updating the website and hoping new customers come and see what you're all about, you can become a publisher and bring them to you. I've seen so many startups and founders hire expensive consultants and go through weeks of company positioning and messaging work only to see none of those messages actually reach anyone. But that all changes if you can harness (and commit to) the power of using social media and become a publisher.

Now you have a framework for your story. You have an explainer. You're good, right? You can just pop that story and explainer up on the website, and you are done. If you have a good story, people will find you.

I wish it were that easy. But even the best stories from the best founders will go nowhere. There is simply too much noise and information out there from every other company in your industry. Unless you actually get out there and *become a publisher*.

Because of social media today, any founder can be a publisher.

While I was at Drift, the company became one of the fastest growing startups of all time. A big part of that growth came because of the brand—the reputation the company had—that we built. And that reputation started through social media.

When I joined Drift, we had no website traffic. No blog traffic. No email subscribers. But we had one key ingredient: a founder with a strong personal brand. David Cancel (@dcancel on Twitter) had built up a following of close to 40,000 followers on Twitter after years of sharing his lessons, learnings, and rants about startups. David was a pro at taking those learnings and distilling them down into witty nuggets for social media. David was also consistent in his social media presence. Building a substantial social media following requires quality, consistency, and frequency. It is not enough to jump in, tweet once a week from the bathroom, and then complain about social media not working. Like anything in life, if you want this to work, you need to make the commitment, and it takes time. David understood that and over time built a loyal following of startup enthusiasts, other founders, and investors. After starting Drift, David shifted more of his content to focus on those lessons as they applied to his new company. So David's followers got a firsthand look at building a new company, as David was "working in public" by sharing what we were doing at Drift in real time online.

Social media often makes founders and CEOs a little uncomfortable. You might not be into the idea of promoting yourself. You might not feel comfortable "thumping your chest" and talking about your company online. You might think you don't have the time to do it. You may think social media is about vanity, but I'm talking about social media for your business. If you care about growing your business, then it is worth taking social media seriously. Used correctly and with a purpose, social media can be a powerful and indispensable tool to build a brand and stand out from the competition. And the value of social media goes far beyond likes and followers. In the example of Drift, David's social media audience was the jumping-off point for our popular podcast *Seeking Wisdom*. *Seeking Wisdom* was the jumping-off point for our annual event HYPERGROWTH, which attracted thousands of attendees and Drift customers from beyond Boston. Social media creates an incredible advantage because of the power to both build an audience and then get real-time feedback from that audience on what they are interested in and what they want more of, which shows you where you should spend your time.

I think the best marketing strategy for any startup in 2022 and beyond is to think about building a media company for your niche—not just "building a marketing team." Today, any business can be their own publisher.

THE POWER OF SOCIAL MEDIA

The power of social media is the reach *anyone* can have globally, without paying a cent for the access, other than the cost (if any) of using the internet. To put it in the context of business: social media allows you to reach your dream customers directly online.

This is a huge shift for marketing. In prior generations, companies or individuals had to raise millions in venture capital dollars, hire a six-figure PR agency, and practically beg for the press to write an article about them—and then have no control over that story (if they were lucky enough to get press at all). Or of course you could pay your way to building an audience and just buy advertising on TV, in print, and on the radio.

But today, the founder of any startup can use social media to build an audience of dream customers online.

And you can do it without being overly promotional and selling your soul. And no, you don't have to post pictures of what you ate for lunch.

There are three keys to becoming a publisher as a founder:

1. Founders should be active and posting at least three to five times a week on social media, specifically on Twitter and LinkedIn.
2. Founders should start a podcast focused on their niche.
3. Founders should make public speaking a priority, whether or not they like it.

We will discuss podcasting and public speaking in subsequent chapters. For now, we are focusing on Twitter and LinkedIn.

First, a caveat. My aim is not to outline every marketing platform or channel here. It's not that it would be impossible, but it would be bad marketing advice because each business has its own particulars. You are better served by learning and starting with a few fundamentals. These are the places that I think are best suited to help you build a brand as a founder. Twitter and LinkedIn give the most return on investment for most founders, and that is where I will focus. I want to give you useful, specific advice. So I'm telling you this: do not try to be everywhere.

Can you build a founder brand through blogging? Or with a newsletter? Or with a YouTube channel? Or on TikTok? Yes. But if you're a founder, you have everything else to do: hiring, training, sales, product, customers, finance, just to name a few. Twitter, LinkedIn, and podcasts (which I'll present later) are the "compound lifts" of social media marketing for founders. Compound lifts are exercises that work multiple muscle groups at the same time—squats, deadlifts, presses, and cleans. These are the things that will give you the most bang for your buck.

One last comment for the skeptical founder here: Now, before you mutter that you really don't want to use social media or you don't have the time, it is OK to use your marketing team to do the posting on your behalf. They can do the posting for you (ideally taking original thoughts from your interviews, internal meetings, or from a dedicated time each week or month where they can pick your brain to ghostwrite social media content for you), but you as the founder must be the person who does the responding to your followers, not your team. And you must be on social media to have your finger on the pulse of what people are saying. We will talk more about the power of personal responses later on in the book.

MOST FOUNDERS STINK AT SOCIAL MEDIA

With social media for founders, the bar is low.

Most founders stink at social media because they don't understand the importance of it and don't prioritize it daily. When they think of it, it is as an afterthought, so they do it in a haphazard and sloppy manner. I want to help you overcome both things right now.

On the importance of social media: no matter your business or your industry, if you sell to people, people are more likely to buy from brands that they know, like, and trust. As the founder of the company, you are the face of the brand. Being active on social media will help you bridge the gap between strangers and customers. And as a marketer, I want to use that to my advantage. Social media is your own PR channel. Social media is the "media arm" of your business.

And by the way, you don't need millions (or even thousands) of followers for social media to be meaningful. It's not about the likes, comments, or retweets. Social media is ultimately about being a part of the insider conversations that are happening in your niche among your dream customers every day online. Can you see how being in the middle of those conversations would give you an advantage?

On not having enough time to do it: make time. Having worked with founders to help build their brands, I know they are all busy. I get it. But I am going to give it to you straight here. There isn't a hack or a shortcut. You simply need to make time to do it. But it doesn't need to be over twenty minutes a day, perhaps even ten. One of the best ways I've found to manage this is how I do anything that I don't want to do, but I need to get done: I put it on the calendar. I work with one startup CEO, and he has a reminder on his calendar every morning to take fifteen minutes and go on Twitter and LinkedIn with the goal of writing a new post, commenting on at least one other post, and reading posts from key players in his industry.

Outside of not seeing the value in it or not having enough time, many founders also struggle with understanding the concept of tailoring the content to the platform. The goal is not to just take the same thoughts and copy and paste them everywhere. Ross Simmonds, CEO of Foundation, has a simple formula that I like to follow: focus on brevity on Twitter and longer posts with a story attached on LinkedIn. Next time you're on those channels, remember those two principles, and you'll see that the more popular content usually falls into those two buckets on Twitter and LinkedIn. Observe what works well for others and see what you can learn from it for your account.

CHAPTER 6

TWITTER AND LINKEDIN

L et's take a minute and talk about why I focus on Twitter and LinkedIn. There are so many channels, why these two? As a founder, Twitter and LinkedIn will give you the best opportunity to succeed with the least resources. They are two places where you can build an audience solely based on the clarity of your thoughts, and it can be done by typing on the keyboard of your phone or laptop. You can build a following with text only. I strongly believe that no matter what industry you are in as a founder, start with Twitter and LinkedIn, and do it well. I think most founders can win on Twitter and LinkedIn.

Both platforms make it easy to follow and connect with other people in your network. Your messages can easily "catch on" simply from a retweet or comment. They make it easy to follow and "listen" to others much bigger than you, so you can learn what great looks like as a model, but also so you can follow the conversation and stay relevant.

These platforms provide you with instant feedback. You get unfiltered direct replies from your connections and customers. These also are platforms where you can see if your targeting of your niche is working, because you will see if your posts are getting responses or not. Remember, the shorter the feedback loop is, the faster you learn.

These platforms, Twitter specifically, also are where the "sneezers" (as Seth Godin calls them) are in any industry. Sneezers are the early adopters: the ones who have authority and influence in your niche and are most likely to spread the message. Twitter is the place for sneezers. It is where the early adopters (in nearly every industry) hang out. Twitter is a much more transactional platform, meaning that you have more immediate reactions to your words and can get almost instant feedback. Plus, given the nature of the Twitter feed, it's an ephemeral channel. Things don't last long. You can post once or ten times a day, and because of the way the Twitter feed works, people don't get "tired" of seeing your stuff over and over, because there's a good chance they might not see it due to fast Twitter moves. This also should lower the barrier for entry in your mind. Take the mindset that most people probably aren't even going to see what you write. So the purpose of posting is to find your voice first.

LinkedIn has changed a lot over the last few years. The thought with LinkedIn used to be that it was for job searching and "professional networking" only. You only accept connections from people you know, and you definitely don't post about what's going on in your day like you would on Twitter. But like all social media channels today, LinkedIn has grown to become a content platform. How I think about LinkedIn now is that it's like *business Twitter*. Instead of potentially anonymous users on Twitter, on LinkedIn, you're reaching people under the company profile and usually with a business context. Career advice, personal development, industry-specific knowledge and observations, leadership lessons, management mantras, work/life balance. Those are examples of the content that works well on LinkedIn.

Especially if you're a B2B, LinkedIn is the single most important platform you need to be spending your time on. I've consistently had LinkedIn posts get 500,000+ views with people I care about inside of sales and marketing (my niche), and I haven't seen that on Twitter. LinkedIn provides an incredible opportunity to reach your dream customers with relevant content. Now, it took me several years to build up an audience of 100,000+ followers on LinkedIn, so I don't expect everyone reading this to post and get 500,000 views on a piece of content. But I can promise you that in most cases, business content will reach more people that you care about than it will on Twitter.

In terms of timing, it took me a decade to reach 20,000 followers on Twitter, but it only took me two years to go from 12,000 followers on LinkedIn to 100,000. Here are the main differences in how I write on LinkedIn versus Twitter:

- My posts are more planned on LinkedIn. I don't post random funny things there, as my followers don't seem to want that.

- I post on LinkedIn once a day, maybe twice, but not more than that. On Twitter, I may post ten times in a day.

- I spend more time replying to people on LinkedIn, strategically, as I can see what company they come from, and therefore, I can target my responses.

- Instead of anonymous accounts on Twitter, LinkedIn has everyone connected to a personal page. There's no better way to reach people at companies and in industries interesting to you than by looking at their LinkedIn personal page.

- Every new connection is someone that opts in to see your content. It isn't a random connection. And this isn't the LinkedIn of the last decade where you "only connect with people you know." I now see LinkedIn as a content platform.

- You can look at their connections and see who you'd like to connect with, as well, and send them an invitation.

- For LinkedIn, I am talking about posts, not articles. Focus on posts, as they will appear in the newsfeed. I rarely use articles. Posts only.

- Overall, my advice is to take content that is popular for you on Twitter (or in other places) and tailor it for LinkedIn. Twitter gives you speed. Things happen fast on Twitter, and you can quickly "test" an idea. Look at the newsfeed, look at posts that are popular, and adapt your writing and start getting your thoughts and ideas in rotation on LinkedIn.

- Twitter performs better with more broad marketing topics for me, but LinkedIn performs better with very specific B2B marketing niches. Target your posts to the platform and to the niche.

- For both platforms, again, write as you speak. Don't be overly formal; if anyone has listened to your podcast, they know exactly what you sound like, and if your posts don't align with that, your credibility will be questioned.

- Short sentences are key! They are easier to understand, and they keep the attention of your audience. Overall, on social media, aim to have your sentences be seven words or less.

- Commenting is a great way to connect with your audience. If they comment on your post or tweet, respond. Respond to every single meaningful engagement you have, especially in the early days of focusing on building out your presence on Twitter and LinkedIn. People want to know that's really you there. It's called social media after all. Social equals a two-way conversation.

- Comments also can expose your content and POV to other people you might not know and people who are not following you.
- Comments can also become the best content to post later on LinkedIn. I know if something is a popular comment it will also be a popular post (and that most people won't have seen the comment, so I'll be reaching new people with the same topic that has already proven successful by using the comment as a post). Pow! I just blew your mind, I know ☺.

Start with Twitter and LinkedIn, but don't exclude other platforms. You can and should be on other platforms relevant to your industry. For example, if you are the founder of a consumer brand, I would expect you to be on Instagram as well. These are just the primary channels because they help you clarify your messages *for* the other platforms.

HOW TO WRITE YOUR LINKEDIN AND TWITTER BIOS

OK, let's talk about your bios for each channel. This seems like a basic detail, but I see many people get it wrong simply by not putting in the effort. Your Twitter and LinkedIn bios are the front door to your presence on social media. They set the context for people who might be interested in following you and let everyone know what you're about. A good bio is clear and specific. This is about setting the right context and setting you up for success.

Step 1: *Make Your Profile Visually Engaging*

A visually engaging profile starts with your profile picture and your cover photo. Below are two examples of LinkedIn pages from founders I've worked with: Ben Jabbawy, CEO at Privy, and David Cancel, CEO at Drift.

The simple formula to follow here is a good headshot and a good background image for both Twitter and LinkedIn. If you don't have a good headshot, get one done. You're

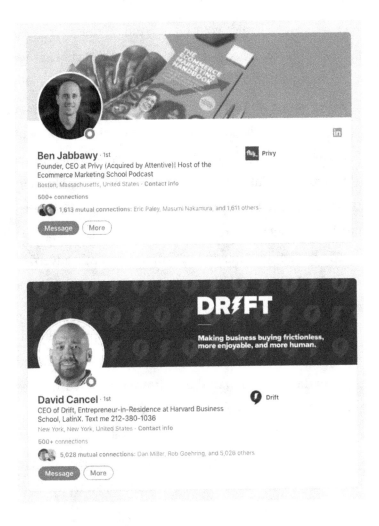

the founder. You are the face of the brand. It's such an easy thing to get a nice headshot done (heck, you can even just take one yourself with your iPhone today) that there's no excuse. My preference is to use a clear and direct headshot for the founder's bio on social media. I know some people use cartoons or graphics, but that doesn't fit me. This is for you. Your social media presence online should represent you. And remember, the entire goal of using social media is to build confidence and get people to know, like, and trust you as the founder through social media. Use a real headshot to show the real you. Not a cartoon.

The background image can promote a subtle advertisement for the brand. Plus, it works as a simple explainer for who you are and what your company does. The Privy and Drift examples above are great and easy to copy. Work with a designer to create something that represents your brand and fits the dimension of the Twitter and LinkedIn cover photos. Don't get lazy and upload a random image here. Spend the design effort to make a professional banner.

As of this writing, the recommended size for the LinkedIn cover photo is 1,584 x 396 pixels, and Twitter is 1,500 x 500 pixels.

Here are a few other examples I like that will give you a sense of what "good" looks like here.

Asia's profile is a good example for consultants or agencies:

John's is a good example for creators, coaches, and trainers:

Another thing I like to have founders (and the entire company) do is update their social media banners to promote products, launches, or upcoming events, like Shopify President Harley Finkelstein is doing here to promote Shopify's annual conference Unite:

You can use the same style for both Twitter and LinkedIn. Just get the dimensions correct.

Step 2: For LinkedIn, Write an Interesting Headline

Your headline should be clear and direct. Here's an example from my profile:

Dave Gerhardt · 1st

CMO at Privy (#1 Sales App on Shopify) | I help B2B startups with
marketing at davegerhardt.com

Talks about #marketing, #copywriting, and #b2bmarketing

Greater Burlington Area · **Contact info**

 Privy

In my headline, I mention I am the CMO (Chief
Marketing Officer) at Privy. But I'm also assuming that
most people on LinkedIn have not heard of Privy. So what
is Privy for those not in the know? It's the number one
sales app on Shopify. I've added social proof and credibility to my profile. Copywriting matters on LinkedIn too.
The more specific you can be, the better.

Now, maybe you have a side hustle like I do with DGMG.
Instead of saying "Founder, DGMG," spice it up a little. In the
same way people don't know Privy, people don't know DGMG.
So instead I lead with the benefits: get help with startup marketing from me. Find a quick value statement about what it
is you do and throw it in there. Titles are too vague, so give
your audience more information about what you actually do.

Asia also nails this:

Asia Orangio · 2nd

SaaS growth consultant   Board Member at Moz   TAG's Up-
and-Coming Marketer of the Year 2019

Atlanta, Georgia, United States · **Contact info**

 DemandMaven

And so does Ben. He even uses this as an opportunity to promote the podcast he hosts:

Ben Jabbawy · 1st
Founder, CEO at Privy (Acquired by Attentive)| Host of the
Ecommerce Marketing School Podcast
Boston, Massachusetts, United States · Contact info

This seems like a minor detail, but it's major. My LinkedIn and Twitter profiles have around 20,000 views each month—each! That is 40,000 visitors a month. That would be good for most websites. Please, please, please, spend the time here and use this valuable real estate in your social media bios to your advantage.

Note: I also am always tweaking the message here. I am always on the lookout for other copy and bios that I like and can take inspiration from. So always be changing and testing the copy here. Especially if you're in a startup, the message is going to change a lot. And social media is a great place to debut your new copy.

Step 3: Show Your Accomplishments on LinkedIn, Not Just Where You Worked and Your Title

These are your facts. This is the work you've done. Use that to your advantage to stand out. I treat my LinkedIn profile as my living, breathing résumé. And not only is it a living document you can update—it's public! Anyone in your industry can see it.

For example:

Drift
4 yrs 2 mos

VP of Marketing
Oct 2015 – Nov 2019 · 4 yrs 2 mos
Greater Boston Area

I joined Drift in October 2015 as employee #8 & the first full-time marketer to jumpstart the company's marketing efforts. During my 4+ years at the company:

- 50,000+ businesses used our product and we grew from $0 to eight-figures in revenue.

- Drift was profiled in the New York Times (Corner Office), TechCrunch, Forbes, Fortune, Harvard Business Review, and 100+ other publications.

- Drift was named to the Forbes Cloud 100, LinkedIn's Top 50 Startups, Entrepreneur's Top Company Cultures, 2018 SaaS Company of the Year by the New England Venture Capital Association, and a finalist for the Boston Business Journal's Best Places to Work.

- We created the category of Conversational Marketing.

- We created our annual conference HYPERGROWTH (which had 12,000+ marketing & sales people registered in two years and became one of the fastest growing business events in the world).

- We wrote the official book on Conversational Marketing published by Wiley (the book was an instant #1 new release on Amazon in the marketing, sales, and commerce categories and a top 20 business book in the United States).

- We created Seeking Wisdom, a popular podcast about personal and professional growth and grew to over 50,000 downloads/month.

Yes, I very easily could have just listed my job titles and the time I spent doing each one of those jobs, but that doesn't tell you a story. I spent four years at Drift doing many things, going through a ton of growth and change, and my bio needs to reflect that. Also, this level of detail shows your engagement and passion for the brand, rather than that you were just along for the ride.

When done right, your LinkedIn profile is like your résumé on steroids. Use it to your advantage.

What if you're a founder and don't need a résumé because you aren't trying to get anyone to hire you? Well, that might be true. But all of your investors, advisors, future customers, future employees, future partners— they are all on LinkedIn, and they want to see how credible you are too. Spend the time on this.

Step 4: Keep Your Twitter Bio Short, Simple, and Direct

It's Twitter, and there is a character limit for a reason. You can't use Twitter to list out all of your accomplishments like you can on LinkedIn, so as a result, I treat the bio differently.

In my Twitter bio, I give all the basic details about my employment history and status, qualifying me as someone who (at least on the surface) knows what I'm talking about. But you'll notice that I have my bio intentionally focused on a niche here: marketing.

Dave Gerhardt
@davegerhardt Follows you

I tweet about marketing. CMO @Privy. Previously @Drift. I help B2B startups with marketing at davegerhardt.com

⊙ Burlington, VT 🔗 davegerhardt.com ▦ Joined October 2009

Do I have interests other than marketing? Of course. Lots of them. But putting the fact that I like to work out, play golf, and spend time with family doesn't add any value to my bio. Those are all things that can come up over time after following me. The purpose of my Twitter account—as I'm letting people know in my bio—is to talk about marketing with marketing people. The niche I am focused on is B2B marketing. And there's no better way to attract like-minded people than letting them know that's what I'm thinking about too.

Consistency is one of the most important ingredients to building a following online. People don't follow me because I tweet about what I'm eating, poetry, politics, sports, or travel. More than 80 percent of my content is about marketing. That doesn't have to be how you use Twitter, but that is how I use Twitter, and it's helped me build an audience that is meaningful for my businesses and brand. If that's what you're after, then this is the strategy I'd recommend. This is not the approach I'd take if I were trying to build a viral meme account. This is the approach I'd take as a founder who wants to get their message out to the world and build a brand.

You can tweet about whatever your heart desires, but in this book, I am trying to teach you how to build a following as a founder. Therefore, this is my recommendation to you: target your tweets to your niche and your industry. If you're the CEO of an SaaS company that sells sales software, make sales your core topic, and tweet 80 percent of the time about sales content.

Step 5: In Both, Be a Curator and Do Your Work in Public

Curating content is the easiest place to start when you're publishing on social media.

What do I mean by this? You need to be a curator by talking about what is going on in your industry and staying up to date with trends. As a founder, you are an expert in your industry, so share that expertise! Talk about what is happening in the industry. Let your audience know and feel that you are sharing tips and information with them that they cannot find anywhere else.

This is the easier one: share insights and interviews from others in your industry; retweet and share interesting perspectives and POVs. You can build an audience without having to create "original" content. But as an industry insider (you're the founder after all), you're probably following interesting accounts, influencers, and people you've worked with in the past.

"Content curation in social media is the premise that you don't actually have to write or produce all of the content that you publish. Curating content is finding the content that your audience will find important or useful, and repositioning that in a way that serves both your organization and your audience." This is from Vala Afshar, Chief Digital Evangelist at Salesforce. Vala has built an incredible audience on Twitter (I say incredible not just because he has over 500,000 followers, but because his content actually gets engagement that is real; he doesn't come off as a robot account just blasting out memes or clickbait), and he's done this mainly as a curator. He often posts other people's content about marketing, leadership, and technology, and that has helped build his brand across those industries.

Vala Afshar Retweeted

Vala Afshar @ValaAfshar · Oct 22, 2020

The greatest enemy of knowledge is not ignorance, it is the illusion of knowledge.

—Stephen Hawking

90 3.5K 13.3K

I always recommended starting as a "curator" because it lowers the barrier for entry and success. And as a founder in a niche, you're most likely already in the middle of this content. You just need to take the next step and share it.

After becoming a curator, the best next step—or level up—is to begin publishing original content. Sorry. You're not going to get out of here thinking you can just magically post quotes from famous people or cat GIFs and build an audience online. You need to actually share your own unique POV. That is what makes social media great; after all, it gives everyone an opportunity to share their authentic voice. The best way to do this is by "working in public."

Talk about what you are doing on a daily basis. You're the founder. You're on calls. In meetings. Hiring. Recruiting. Talking to partners. Thinking about the roadmap. Trying to conquer the next big challenge. That is the best content you could share with people outside of your company. Reality TV is the best marketing strategy. People don't want the highly produced corporate speak from your social media account. They want you! You're using social media to get people to know, like, and trust you, after all. That will not happen by just tweeting about the stock price or the latest local business journal award your company won. Share what's going on as you're going through it.

Think back to that almost-catastrophe of still using lead forms at Drift and how David Cancel did his work in public by posting about the problem and how we resolved it. We shared the whole backstory, not just the finished product. And then we began sharing what we were doing at Drift as we were doing it. Pictures from events. Pictures from the road. Tweets about new things we were doing at Drift that weren't available to the public yet. Doing your work in public is the corporate form of reality television. It isn't edited or filtered. It may be ugly or embarrassing (well, hopefully not ugly and embarrassing, because I don't think you should be putting everything on social media, but you get what I mean), but you are giving your followers a glimpse into your reality with the goal of earning trust and credibility back online.

Gary Vaynerchuk, entrepreneur and social media expert, advises founders to not worry about creating *new* content each day on social media; instead, just document what happens each day. He suggests talking about the meetings you had, what advisors suggested, and hints about things to come. He calls it "document, don't create," and I think it's the best strategy a founder could use to build a brand online.

What should you post? Post about conversations in-house and ideas you have for new products. Post about missteps and celebrations. Post about your process—for example, how you get ready for events or meetings. Some of my best content has come when I share my process for writing, or how I structure my day, or how important walks are for creativity. You get it. Look, there are a handful of different ways to go about "doing your work in public," but whatever path you take, the most important piece is that it feels authentic to you. This should be natural, not scripted.

For example, if I were Dave, the founder of a new marketing agency, I could be sharing updates about new clients we've landed, interesting learnings and trends from meetings, new strategies we're testing, and quotes and snippets from things I'm reading, watching, and listening to. All of this (and you can do it in a way without sharing confidential information about your company) can work like a magnet to build an audience of your dream customers. Social media has a great way of attracting like-minded people based on what you publish, and you can use this to your advantage by doing your work in public or "documenting" what you're doing. This isn't about tweeting pictures of your breakfast, though. It's about conveying expertise and providing value to your audience (and as a result, you build trust and earn followers in your niche).

Amanda Goetz is the founder of House of Wise (luxury CBD and a community for women) and a great example to follow of a founder who has an engaged audience on social media and has used "working in public" as a way to create social media content, from teasing new product launches:

Amanda Goetz ✓
@AmandaMGoetz

New @house__of__wise product launching in 2 weeks.

Can't wait to share this one with you all!!

❤ ❤ ❤ ❤ ❤ ❤

3:39 PM · Aug 2, 2021 · Twitter Web App

To sharing her personal productivity lessons:

Amanda Goetz ✓
@AmandaMGoetz

Productivity hack:
1. take call notes in an email
2. end call 5 mins early
3. send follow ups / recaps before you move to the next task

9:58 AM · Apr 5, 2021 · Twitter Web App

Amanda Goetz ✓
@AmandaMGoetz

Reminder: focus on moving forward 2-3 impactful items today.

Quality work > quantity of emails answered

9:26 AM · Aug 2, 2021 · Twitter for iPhone

To sharing her personal life lessons:

Amanda Goetz ✓
@AmandaMGoetz

Replying to @AmandaMGoetz

Make sure your life OKRs are measuring the right things.

Personal Example:
"get married" is a dangerous life objective

"Find someone that you are excited to do life with" will lead to a more successful outcome.

9:26 AM · Jul 27, 2021 · Twitter for iPhone

Amanda Goetz ✓
@AmandaMGoetz Follows you

Founder, @house__of__Wise (luxury CBD + community for women) | Single mom x 3 | Midwest ➡ MIAMI

⊙ New York 𝒮 houseofwise.co/?ref=samtackeff 🎂 Joined March 2009

4,300 Following **41.8K** Followers

Followed by Lauren Hall, Marketing Brew ☕, and 57 others you follow

Over time, these all work as magnets to attract like-minded people to Amanda's profile (and back to the Twitter bio and why this matters), where they will be able to learn more about who she is and what she's doing.

And there's another great example of a social bio and cover photo too.

PRINCIPLES FOR BOTH TWITTER AND LINKEDIN

Become your industry's curator and do your work in public—these two principles increase your chances for becoming known as an expert in your field, the founder other people look to as a role model. Curating entails creating and reposting industry news and trends from respected sources, while your work in public includes building, hiring, and growth, but not just company stuff; include what you're reading, listening to, and watching. This working and living in public attracts like-minded people.

As discussed before, use commenting as a strategy. Reply to everyone—really, *everyone*. Especially in the early days. I have abandoned this strategy personally now because I can't keep up, but in the early days I would try to respond to every meaningful comment, and I encouraged other founders to do the same.

The following page has a great example of a founder using a comment on his post to create a connection. Gil Allouche is the founder at Metadata, a B2B SaaS company. He could have easily just left and never commented. But then he'd look like most other founders on LinkedIn just posting links and leaving and never actually contributing to the discussion. He's focused on building his brand using LinkedIn, so he's committed to commenting and adding value with his content.

And the best part about Gil's response is that now it can be used as more LinkedIn content. He can take his comment and repurpose it for a future post and increase who will see it (and he already has a good feeling that this topic is valuable to others since it came up organically from his original post).

You don't have to comment with twenty sentences every time, but it does make a big difference every now and then when you can hop in on your own post and reply in the comments. In addition to the long, thoughtful responses, you can also just quickly hop in and give people

Gil Allouche • 1st
Founder & CEO at metadata.io (*we're hiring!*)
23h • 🌐

Great read for founders & CEOs thinking about Series B

https://lnkd.in/d3AyJZ3

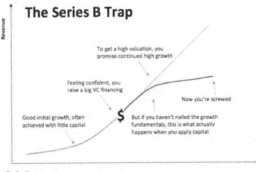

The Series B Trap

To get a high valuation, you
promise continued high growth

Feeling confident, you
raise a big VC financing

Now you're screwed

Good initial growth, often
achieved with little capital

But if you haven't nailed the growth
fundamentals, this is what actually
happens when you apply capital

🔵🔵😊 155 · 28 comments

👍 Like   💬 Comment   ↪ Share   ✈ Send

Most relevant ▼

Amir Reiter • 1st   20h •••
On a Mission To Help 10,000 Businesses Get Work Done Better, Fa...

What would your advice be to other Entrepreneurs in reference to
raising money from VCs.

Like · 🔵 2 | Reply · 4 Replies

Gil Allouche `Author`   20h •••
Founder & CEO at metadata.io (*we're hiring!*)

Oh man - my biggest advice would be to find an investor
who truly believes in you and where you can take the
business, an investor you cannot wait to pick up the phone
and call when you are having a tough day, a dilemma or just
good news to share -- and have a meaningful, authentic
conversation without a transaction on the table. When you
find them - sign a term sheet even if the valuation is not the
highest. In *my(order of priority:

1. Partner <-- most important.
2. VC
3. Terms
4. Valuation

Like · 🔵😊💙 6 | Reply

a fist bump, high five, or a quick word. The simple act of acknowledgment goes a long way.

I also advise this strategy on *other* people's content too. You should be actively seeking out the influencers and "sneezers" in your industry and adding your thoughts in the comments of their content. You'll be surprised at how much exposure your content can get from commenting on the content of others—even if it's just an attempt at wit or humor like I did on the following page.

Andy Raskin is an influencer in my space (B2B marketing), and he's someone who I know has the ears of people I'd also get value from being in front of. So I try to comment on his stuff frequently. And the result was a comment that got more engagement on its own than Andy's post. This is not even a flex on Andy (hey Andy), but it's a great example of the power of commenting on other people's posts and how it can result in you—your profile—being shown to hundreds and thousands of other people in your niche.

Remember how I talked about turning comments into posts? LinkedIn knows this now too. They even started prompting me to turn some popular comments into original posts. (You can see this instruction in the previous

Everyone gets 1-star reviews

8:19 AM

Hey Andy, Recently took charge as a Chief Sales Officer of ▓▓▓▓ Need to understand what can be done to take ▓▓▓ to a global stage and increase it to multi fold valuations ▓▓▓

Andy Raskin joined the conversation from View post 6:19 AM

Andy Raskin 9:41 AM
Hi ▓▓▓ thanks for reaching out, and congratulations on your new role. Not sure I can help, but maybe check out a few of my posts:

- http://bit.ly/greatest-sales-deck

- http://bit.ly/namethenewgame

Your recent messages have been sent via email 9:43 AM

10:37 AM • Email reply
Thanks Andy. Was interesting but need more in depth insights. Appreciate the help. ▓▓▓▓▓▓▓▓▓▓▓▓

👍 😊 🙌 135 · 32 comments

👍 Like   💬 Comment   ➡ Share   ✈ Send

Add a comment...   😊   🖼

Most relevant ▼

Dave Gerhardt • You   1mo (edited) •••
CMO at Privy (acquired by Attentive) | I help startups with marketi...

Hey Andy in one line over chat tell me how I can triple the valuation of my company and then I'll let you know if I think you're good enough to maybe help us.

Like · 👍 🙌 😊 140 | Reply · 9 Replies

Lead the conversation by turning your comment into a post.   ✕
Share this post.

103

screenshot.) They know that comments are a great way to find what content will land with an audience. If it worked in the comments, it would work as a post and oftentimes reach even more people.

Outside of those two main principles, the following tips will help you create successful Twitter and LinkedIn practices:

- Find great and model great.
  - Be curious online in your niche and find people worth following.
- Appearance matters.
  - Make sure to set your profile picture and cover photo.
  - Use Twitter's Pinned Tweet and LinkedIn's Featured section to your advantage.
    - Each platform gives you a way to highlight a top piece of content on your profile a.k.a. your homepage.

Amanda uses her pinned tweet to boost the credibility of her company, highlighting a recent fundraising announcement for everyone to view when they land on her profile on Twitter.

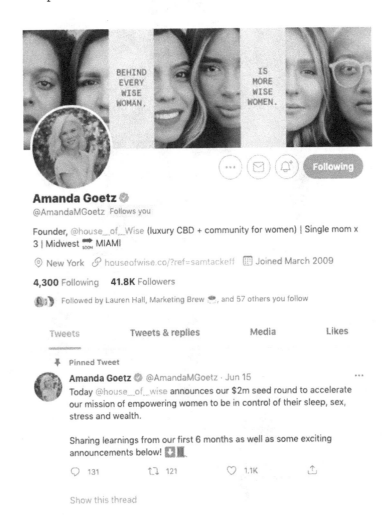

Hiten uses this to tell a story, which draws people in to learn more about his company.

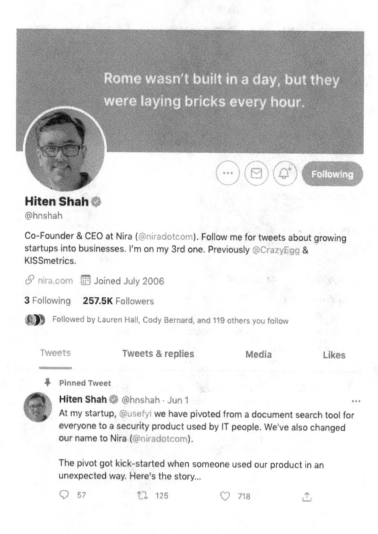

Here's an example of LinkedIn Featured posts high-lighted on my profile. Both are videos that were popular on LinkedIn and subtly promote DGMG, so I picked those to highlight because that type of content will be relevant and interesting to people who come across my profile.

- Focus on your topics.
  - Define one or two core areas of focus, for example, startups and marketing.
  - Personal stories about those areas of focus will captivate your followers. This is the "do your work in public" part.
- There are two ways to get followers: education and entertainment.

- Most will try too hard to be entertaining—not a good fit.
- Instead, focus on education. Any founder can educate.
- Edutainment is the holy grail, when you can both educate and entertain.
- Show consistent clarity of thought. Great copy wins online.
- Compress ideas down into 280 characters for Twitter.
- Present in a quick and readable way; remember that everyone is scanning, and you want them to read your material.
- Be a contrarian. Be different. The feed is noisy. Strong opinions stand out.
- Consistency is key. Daily is when it will really take off.
- First, find your voice. Remember that that goal is not to build a following overnight. This will take time. Treat the first weeks and months as "finding your voice" as opposed to worrying about how many followers you have. You need to learn what to

say, how to say it, and what people are interested in. Be patient and publish regularly.

- Participate.
  - You gotta be there. You need to do it yourself, or at least all of the comments and responses need to come from the founder directly. Plus, you need to actually be there in the middle of conversations to have a sense of what people in your industry are interested in. This is the advantage social media gives you, but you have to put in the time. Scheduling a bunch of tweets and having the intern manage the replies is not going to build your audience. You will spend time there.
  - Comment and respond.
  - Always be curious. See what content is getting people talking. Be a consumer. It's tough to know what to say if you're not regularly listening to others.

FREQUENCY

As we have discussed, you need to be on both of these platforms every single day. A daily check-in gives you the information you need to learn and share. ClickFunnels Founder Russell Brunson wrote in his book *Dotcom Secrets*, "Publishing daily is important because you will quickly see what topics and ideas people respond to and what they don't. Soon you'll become better at creating and posting things that people care about most. As you do that, your audience will grow, you will become more confident, and your message will become clear."

Showing up every day lets people know you are for real, which is one of your goals as a founder, but it also helps you find your voice. Where would you learn more: from publishing 52 times in a year (once a week) or from publishing 365 times (every day)? More is better. Post often, but be patient.

FOLLOW YOUR DREAM FOLLOWERS FIRST

One of the great things about social media is that it's not always a one-way street. Yes, you'll need your dream followers to come follow you if you want them to see your content, but you can first go and follow them. This doesn't guarantee they will follow you back on Twitter or accept your invitation, but it's worth a try and costs you nothing. If they do follow and connect, then they've then opted in to see your content in your feed, which is the ultimate goal.

Start by making a list of the top five, ten, fifty, or even one hundred people you think should be following you and connect with them via your platforms of choice.

Plus, this helps you keep a finger on the pulse of your industry. You need to know what is going on, and social media is like a cheat code for becoming an insider. If you're following the right people, every time you go on Twitter and LinkedIn you should be seeing relevant conversations and content from your industry.

WHAT ABOUT HASHTAGS?

My editors really wanted me to answer this question, but for the sake of this book, hashtags are not relevant. Yes, they do serve a purpose on Twitter, but it's most for following major news topics or live events. And yes, you can use them on LinkedIn, but I haven't ever seen them have an impact. And the last thing I want is to have people who read my book go back to social media and starting writing posts like: "Always be closing #closing #sales #selling #marketing."

So, skip the hashtags. Focus on the content.

YOUR TURN

Do you already have social media accounts? Do you have company or brand specific accounts? If so, great. If not, it's time to get them. But I hope you put this book down a few pages ago and took care of that already.

The steps:

1. Get your Twitter and LinkedIn visuals right: update your headshot and add a cover photo for each.

2. Update your Twitter and LinkedIn bios as explained previously. Copy and innovate on a few examples from the book.

3. Set a goal of posting something every day for the next week. If you can't get to it daily, pick three

days this week and commit to them and build off of that the next week.

4. Respond to every single person who comments, likes, or shares your posts.

5. As you grow more comfortable with the platforms, start posting more frequently, always making sure that your content is timely, relevant, and interesting.

6. Decide what time of day you can consistently dedicate yourself to your social media presence, and put it on your calendar as a nonnegotiable, sacred block of time. Make sure that your staff understands this time is sacred and doesn't try to take the time from you.

7. Tweet at me @davegerhardt and let me know you are reading this book right now ☺.

CHAPTER 7

START A PODCAST

After social media, a podcast is the single best channel to build a brand as a founder today. Having a podcast is like being the producer of your own radio station in your niche—without any of the costs or headaches of starting a radio station. And as I'm writing it, I'm realizing that that point doesn't even *matter* because it's 2021 and you, like me, get most of your audio content from podcasts, not the radio.

PodcastHosting.com reports that as of the end of 2020, more than 50 percent of all households in the United States report that they listen to podcasts. Even more amazing, they report that 37 percent of Americans (more than a hundred million people) listen to podcasts every month. As a founder, why wouldn't you want part of that huge audience?

Most people listen to podcasts on their phones, and mostly through two apps: Apple Podcasts and Spotify. And the incredible part is that those apps are on millions (probably billions, but I'm not a math guy) of phones around the world. And I guarantee you that regardless of what products or services you're selling, your dream customers are out there right now listening to podcasts on their phones. To put it a different way: you could literally be in your dream customer's pocket (and ears if they have their headphones in). And that's why podcasting has become my favorite brand-building channel today.

I started my first podcast in 2014. As an avid user of social media, I tweeted my thoughts about those podcasts I was devouring, specifically that while there were a lot of them about how businesses had started, Boston was sorely unrepresented in the shows. I shared that I wondered why that was, and my audience suggested I start a podcast about startups in Boston.

I did.

Within a year of starting my podcast, I went from being a no-name young guy working in a startup in Boston as an account manager to having interviewed more than sixty of the city's most influential founders and built an audience of my own. Not only did I get to spend one-on-one time for an hour with CEOs who I could potentially work with in the future in some capacity, but I now had built my own mini-brand and an audience that I owned: my podcast was downloaded 60,000 times, and I built up an email list of 3,000 subscribers in the Boston startup community.

Starting a podcast was the single best thing I did to help build my brand and launch my career. I never set out to build a brand, had no idea I was doing it at the time, and it all started with a podcast.

WHY A PODCAST?

Pick a product. Pick an industry. There is more competition and noise than ever before. Many businesses do essentially the same thing as their competitors. The marketing among them is similar. The features are similar.

The pricing is similar. So, with that being said, how do you make your company stand out from the competition? The best way is to create a personal relationship with those potential customers and improve their lives in some way, whether that's making them smarter, healthier, better cooks, or better parents.

You build that relationship and trust with people by creating and growing a founder brand. The best way to communicate the founder brand? Podcasting! In podcasting, you are creating content and creating a community because the medium is your *voice*. It's actually you. A real person, building a real business.

Plus, a podcast is a singular way for you, as the founder, to scale your message across all of your channels. It's not just that actual episode, it's all the ways an individual episode can be used in this process, because it all starts with your audio and your ideas. Your episode can become a blog post, turning your audio into a written form. You can extract quotes or clips, and they become your posts on social media. It becomes a Twitter thread, LinkedIn posts, and audio or video clips. It is doing one thing that can then be used in a multitude of ways on different platforms, all building your network, showing who you are, what you stand for, and what you can do for your customers. It builds your network without having to reinvent content for different platforms.

Think about the old way of doing things: for example, just having a blog. You open that Google Doc and stare at the blank page. When you have the post ready, you publish it there, and maybe you share it out on other platforms, but it is static.

A podcast can be used in almost unlimited ways. Written snippets from the podcast can be used as tweets. Longer transcriptions can be used on LinkedIn. If you video yourself as you record, you can take snippets of video and use them as teasers. Each time you do these things, your audience reacts, and that can build content for your next episode.

One podcast episode can give you your social media posts for most of the week.

An often overlooked and critical benefit of having a podcast is that you completely and totally control the podcast, which allows for a very direct relationship with your audience. Even in other forms of connection, specifically your social media accounts, there is a distance between you and your followers. With a podcast, the conversation is truly just between you and that one person who is dedicating their time to listen to your melodious voice and your thoughts. It is a magical thing and carries immense potential for you as a founder.

When asked about the importance of podcasting, David Cancel of Drift said, "I've leveraged podcasting and social media to build my own brand by starting from my principles, which is the idea that when you are talking to and connecting with someone, all of those interactions, every episode that they hear, every tweet that they read, every blog post that they read is essentially increasing the likeliness of that person being connected to you."

Think about that.

He continued, "By embracing social media and podcasting and taking the time to invest in creating content in these various avenues, the relationship that I have with these people increases."

He smiled. "Then, you are able to use those relationships to drive business results."

By having a podcast, you create a direct connection to the brains of your potential customers. For the time they are listening to you, you have their undivided attention, which in our busy world is hard to do otherwise.

GETTING STARTED

Lucky for you and me, the benefits of starting a podcast are big, and the effort to create one today is small thanks to technology and the rise of podcast hosting platforms. But before we get into the details, you have to decide on the goal of your podcast and ask yourself these questions:

- **What is your unique expertise?** As a restaurant owner, can you start a podcast about what it's like running a restaurant today? As a startup founder building a CBD brand, can you interview other founders and people in the industry and share their stories? As a founder in the finance world, can you help educate people on crypto, DeFi, and the future of finance?

- **What other shows exist out there with that expertise?** What gap can you fill? What is already being talked about in the market? Are there existing shows that people listen to? What can you learn from them and take for your show?

- **How will you be different?** Just like your product, your podcast needs a differentiator too. What's the hook for your show?

As you plan episodes, remember that you need to both share your expertise in your particular industry and also let the audience see glimpses of the real you. As you know, humans crave relationships, and if all your podcast does is give them industry information, they may instead turn to other channels. This is an opportunity to actually show your personality. What if you become the show about industry information, but you're the ones who tell it like it really is, and you have rotating guests on each week, like a talk show? While the content of the podcast is of course important, many people listen because of the host. Think about the shows you listen to. You keep coming back because of the host and how their personality is woven into the show. That should be your goal. Don't become a robot reading a script in your podcast—make it you.

There are, of course, key format details that you'll want to think about before launching:

- What is the format? Will it just be you talking?
    - Will you interview guests?
    - In person? Over Zoom remotely?
- How long do you want each episode to be?
- How often can you commit to putting an episode out there? Can you block time weekly on your calendar to record new episodes?
- What is the name of your podcast going to be?
- What is your logo going to be?
- Will you have a music clip to start each episode?
- Will you have an intro read at the beginning of each show? And an outro read?

The next step is to actually start your own podcast. So let's explore each of the steps needed to go from idea to getting your podcast published and available on places like Apple Podcasts and Spotify.

LENGTH AND FREQUENCY OF EPISODES

The length of each episode of your podcast is up to you, but you should be consistent and have a rough idea going in (because you've thought about what type of podcast you want to create).

Ben Jabbawy of Privy uses very short episodes but does them daily. His episodes are only five to ten minutes long—and that's also exactly why they work so well.

When I came to Privy, one of the first channels we launched was a podcast. It was initially called the *Ecommerce Marketing Show* (because that was the niche Privy wanted to own). I started off as the host. It was an interview show (we recorded over Zoom) where I chatted with e-commerce founders and industry experts each week for about forty-five minutes. The show went well, but it felt like something was missing. We had been hearing from our audience that what people liked most were the short, tactical "how-to" nuggets about how to actually *do* the thing in marketing, not just interviewing a guest. So we decided to completely flip the show. We brought in Ben (the founder and CEO) to host, and we decided to do a *daily* five-minute podcast called *Ecommerce Marketing School*. The show took off. And the best part was we didn't need high production or crazy edits to make it work. It was the expert, the founder, Ben, sharing his thoughts for five minutes a day in our industry. The team at Privy eventually got the recording down to a science where Ben didn't actually have to record an episode each day to hit the daily podcast publishing schedule: a few times a month he would block off an hour and batch record episodes. The team kept a running list of topics and ideas that they collaborated with Ben on, and he'd pull that up and record.

Ben hosting *Ecommerce Marketing School* is a great role model for anyone reading this book who wants to build a founder brand. The podcast helped boost Privy's audience. The podcast helped boost customer loyalty. The podcast helped boost Ben's social media presence as it gave him something to talk about nearly every single day.

For Privy, this short form works, and their reach has grown exponentially over time. For your brand, you may want to do a short-form episode model, or you may want to do a longer episode, and do it weekly. David Cancel's podcasts are longer in duration and more formalized in their approach. He publishes one episode a week. He records one new episode a week. It gets added to a backlog of episodes. Rinse and repeat. All of this can be set up into an easy, repeatable system. At Drift with *Seeking Wisdom*, our system was simple: David showed up at the scheduled time to record each week, and the team would do the rest. I would play "host" and prep and develop the titles and topics for each episode and often interview David. After each episode, the podcast audio would be edited by our in-house creative team. (In the beginning we hired an audio editor on Fiverr.)

Regardless of the path you choose, consistency will be the motor that causes your show to grow—not the length of your episodes. To meet your goal of becoming number one in your niche, you must be consistent. This means that you need to decide how often you will release episodes and commit to that schedule. Many podcasters like Ben will record several episodes at a time, so they have a stack of them ready to release on the correct dates. I also like to leave time for that moment when inspiration strikes. It's a great satisfaction to have an exciting idea and record and publish a timely podcast, but inspiration doesn't always strike on recording day, so having a backlog of episodes ready to publish is the key to consistency. When I was hosting a podcast at Drift, I was going out of the office for a month for sabbatical, and we had recorded enough episodes in advance that we didn't miss a single week. I came back from sabbatical, and we got right back to filling up the backlog again.

Weekly episodes seem to be the most effective to stay in your listeners' minds and ears. Or you might prefer the short and daily cadence. Either way, you must be consistent and reliable so your audience can trust that new content will arrive on schedule.

WHAT DO I NEED TO DO A PODCAST?

First you need ideas. Not just ideas, but *content* ideas. Some of your ideas will come from feedback on your social media (assuming you're putting relevant content out into the world that your dream customers would find interesting), but also glean content topics from the community surrounding you. Privy uses their Monday morning Customer Support Team meetings as a source of podcast ideas. They openly discuss questions and ideas from clients and use them as content suggestions. But also remember: as the founder, you are living this every day. You're talking to customers, partners, investors, advisors, analysts, influencers. This is all material that can be used to guide your podcast. You're already talking and thinking about this stuff every day; all I'm asking you to do here is to document it and record it for your podcast.

You will also need equipment for your podcast. Many great podcasts started with nothing more than an iPhone. I have recorded many podcasts just solo ranting in my car, on my iPhone, using the Voice Memos app. I've taken that audio and posted it directly to my podcast with no production. This works if the content is valuable and relevant. For example: I have experience as a marketer, and I am comfortable ranting about marketing solo in my car on my phone. My audience knows me well enough that they are not there because of the production value like an NPR style podcast, but because it's me and they believe I might have something interesting to say about marketing that can help their business. But I've also recorded in my car and then had the audio edited, added music, etc. You can go either path, and the quality of the iPhone (as long as you're in a quiet space) is so good today that you don't need much else. But if you're aiming for a more produced show, even if it just means having guests to interview, there are certain pieces of equipment that will make your podcast sound better to your listeners and help you produce a more consistent and outstanding podcast. If you're doing remote interviews, you can record the interview on your computer over Zoom or using tools like Zencastr and Riverside.fm, which offer a bit more for podcasts. And you'll want to get a good microphone—a USB mic will do the trick for almost everyone. Two great options here are the Blue Yeti mic or, if you want to take a step up, you can get the Shure MV7. If you're doing in-person interviews, you'll need something like the Zoom H4n Pro and Shure SM58 microphones. If you're gear shopping, take these recommendations and plug them into YouTube and watch a few videos from some podcast gearheads to back me up. I am not an audio expert. But I would say this: start small. The gear will not make or break your success. Get something that works and start creating. You can always upgrade your gear down the road as your podcast show is a massive success.

After selecting a mic, you will need a headset, recording software, editing software or service (like a freelancer on Upwork), and a service to publish your podcast (like Libsyn or Transistor.fm).

EDITING YOUR EPISODES

Ben Jabbawy shared his thoughts about the editing process by saying this: "It's highly unlikely that the reason your podcasts fail is because of the quality of the production. It's way more likely it fails because you as the founder just don't commit and don't turn it into a habit."

The most important thing is to have great content and to produce it consistently, but editing is a part of the process. We all know podcasts that are recorded on an iPhone, like mine that I mentioned earlier, with no special editing at all. And for those podcasters, the low-tech, down-and-dirty recording is part of their identity. That's not the case for everyone, nor do I recommend it for everyone.

For most founders looking to start a podcast, I would think about this. You want to exude professionalism and also show your audience that you care enough about their listening time to make a show that sounds like it matters to you and, hopefully, to them. While I don't believe editing makes or breaks the success of our show in the long run, I *do* I think it can go a long way in elevating your brand from the beginning. If it sounds more legit, people will think it's more legit. Period.

Some people have the time and skills to do the audio editing themselves (I knew a founder who loved music and wanted to edit his own stuff), but for the most part, I recommend hiring someone to do it. There are many reputable service providers, such as my friend Erik Jacobson's company Hatch, who can help with this consistently, or you can find someone for one or two episodes on sites such as Fiverr and Upwork. I've had a lot of success there for roughly $50 an episode.

As you think about editing, make sure your editing and production is consistent with the "feel" of your podcast. For example, if you are doing informal five- to ten-minute daily episodes, your editing should just clean up the sound quality and add in the music but not make it sound overproduced or stuffy. By the same token, if you are trying for a more formalized, longer form podcast, make sure the editing and production shows off the level of care you are striving to show.

RELEASING YOUR EPISODES

Once you have recorded your podcast episodes, you will need to use a hosting site to publish your podcast and then get an RSS feed that will allow you to add your show to all of the popular podcast players like Spotify, Apple Podcasts, Stitcher, Google Podcasts, and more. My personal recommendation to clients is to use www.transistor. fm ($19/month) for hosting, as it is a great value and easy to use, and I know many people have used Libsyn over the years.

Using Transistor as a model, when you've taped the episode, you upload your audio file to the site. You name the episode, giving it a title. Your podcast host, in this case Transistor, will have clear instructions on how to submit your podcast to Apple and Spotify. (Just follow the instructions there; it's as easy as copying and pasting a link, I promise.) It's worth noting that it can take twenty-four to forty-eight hours after you submit your podcast to podcast players for it to actually show up, so make sure to factor that into your timeline to launch (basically, don't tell people your show is launched until it's actually available on Apple and Spotify, meaning you can pull it up on your phone and find it).

Knowing how busy every founder is, I know it is a commitment to do regular podcasts (just like exercise and eating right, the answer is simple, not easy). Again, I'd stress that before you release your first episode, you have at least three others ready to release on schedule. And ideally you just begin recording weekly and build up weeks of backlogged episodes.

Just like the importance of social media and building that into your weekly schedule, you must do the same for your podcast. A podcast is like a vegetable garden. Watered and weeded regularly, tended to with care, it will thrive. Without that regular attention, a podcast will react like a garden: the weeds that are the competitors will overtake your plants, and your seedlings will rot. Persistence and consistency will be better than perfection. Set a recording schedule and stick to it.

Set a schedule to record and release episodes. Put it in your weekly schedule, and task someone on your team with holding you accountable to that schedule (here's looking at you, marketing team; the content team inside of marketing should own production of the founder's podcast).

PROMOTING YOUR PODCAST

There also are many ways in which you can promote your podcast using marketing and advertising, but if you have a strong following on social media, and are putting out a relevant and engaging podcast on a consistent basis, it should grow without spending a lot of money on advertising. Actually, scratch that: you shouldn't be spending on advertising to promote your show. That is the whole point of being active on social media and building up a following there. This is your listening audience. The power of building an audience is that you *then have* people to launch to.

You are going to enlist your existing network to help grow your show. Those Twitter followers? Get them on board as early listeners to your podcast. You can even offer them perks to be early subscribers. You can do this with no budget: In the early days of *Seeking Wisdom*, David Cancel and I would regularly shout out Twitter followers who tweeted at us on the show (which felt good; it's cool to hear your name). Gary Vaynerchuk did something similar on Twitter, but instead of just shouting out listeners who tweeted about his podcast, he picked a few listeners to actually record into a future podcast, which created an amazing moment for a fan to get their name in front of his audience. With *Seeking Wisdom*, we also frequently did giveaways (T-shirts, stickers, event tickets) for listeners, and when we did things like book reviews, we'd even buy copies of the books we reviewed for listeners who shared the show on social media. Giveaways work so well because you get basically a two for one. Someone is going to share your show to get the thing you're giving away like a book, T-shirt, or sticker. But then when they *get* their book, T-shirt, or sticker, they are most likely going to take a picture, tag you/your show, and post it on Twitter and other social networks. Now you can see how the power of having a following on social media starts to compound. If you really want to grow your show, I would much rather you take the dollars and budget you would use on "advertising" and do things like this to grow the show organically and give yourself the opportunity to catch on virally through social media.

Before you release an episode, tweet and post on LinkedIn about it. Give the title, any information about guests if you have them, and a hint of the content, and all the links to your podcast, Twitter, LinkedIn, website, and any other platforms. One of my go-to moves here is to take a screenshot of the Zoom interview as we're record-ing the episode and then post it on social media with a recap after and say something like: *had a great conversation with XYZ name today. We talked about topics on ABC. This episode will be available on X date.* This is a great example of building up hype and demand for an episode before it's even published, plus tagging in your guest allows you to tap into their network to promote the show.

Here's an example from a pre-release teaser I did. Here I actually took bulleted notes on a Trello card during the interview and took a screenshot to tease the episode:

Dave Gerhardt @davegerhardt · Jun 29   ···
Good one with @TheCoolestCool recorded today.

open.spotify.com/show/0Rkfao3Zs...

≡ **Description** Edit

Is Clubhouse Dead? Ranking Our Social Media Channels, & Why You Need To
Reply The Hits (with Ross Simmonds, CEO, Foundation)

Venmo
Jack Dorsey & Jay-Z
Marc Benioff
The power of staying top of mind
Replay the hits! Or remix them
PGA Tour advertising
Commenting as a strategy
Is Clubhouse dead?
Ranking our top social media channels
Why Building an audience on social media is a cheat code for business

Another move I like works as a great way to promote
your upcoming episode but also to source questions from
social media for the interview, like this from Sam Parr
below. This works especially well as a teaser if your podcast guest is well known, of course.

Sam Parr   ···
@theSamParr

.@garyvee **on the pod tomorrow.**

What should we ask?

5:27 PM · Aug 5, 2021 · Twitter Web App

I also like to do this solo and will often ask my followers on Twitter, LinkedIn, and my private Facebook group for burning marketing questions they have that I could answer on an upcoming podcast episode.

Post-release, tweet and post quotes, video clips, and links to more in-depth information. Keep your audience engaged and connecting with you through a variety of platforms. It is table stakes to at least promote a new podcast episode once. The standard should be to let people know when a new episode is out. But Twitter and LinkedIn move so fast that you can't assume that promoting an episode once will work to get people to hear about your show, so I like to mix it up. I'll post a text post with a link the day a new podcast is released, like this:

Dave Gerhardt
@davegerhardt   ...

New podcast with @TheCoolestCool is up.
Venmo. Jack. Jay. Benioff. PGA Tour. Clubhouse. Plus we ranked our top social media channels as of today.

Is Clubhouse Dead? Ranking Our Social Media Channels, ...
Listen to this episode from The DGMG Podcast on Spotify.
Ross Simmonds (@thecoolestcool) is the Founder & CEO ...
🔗 open.spotify.com

And then a few days later I'll follow it up with a video clip. I will make notes during the interview of "quotable" moments (things I think will be interesting or controversial on social media to get people talking):

Dave Gerhardt
@davegerhardt

⋯

"I haven't been on Clubhouse in 3 months" -
@thecoolestcool

The real answer is in the last 3 seconds of this video.

I work with a video editor (this is someone I've worked with for a while now, and we have a system down and routines together) and just send her the timestamp of the quote and the headline that I want, and we've created a style for these clips that works well. There are many ways to create the video clips. You can find an editor on Fiverr or work with someone you already know. You can come up with branding that matches your show. But the most important ingredient is the actual clip. The clip needs to be interesting. The clip should cut through the noise. The clip acts as a trailer for your show and will help to drive people to go and listen to full episodes. This is also why I recommend having video "on" when recording your podcast, even if you don't have plans to use the full video. Clips are the best way to consistently promote your podcast.

Another way to promote your podcast is to invite other podcasters to your show. Ultimately the best podcast promotion is not a magic video clip or some secret marketing tactic: it's about getting guests with bigger names. I never listened to the Joe Rogan podcast until he had a controversial interview with Elon Musk.

I never listened to Marc Maron's podcast until he had Barack Obama on the show. I am not expecting you to be able to get Elon Musk and Barack Obama, but I am using them to illustrate a point. Until people know you, they will come for the guests. So if you have an industry with lots of interesting characters, bring them on your podcast. This advice should not be confused with "get controversial people onto your show." My advice here is about expanding your audience by tapping into the name and brand of others. This could be an interesting author or doctor or expert in your space. As they come on and talk on your podcast, you will be reaching a new audience because people now are not there for you, they are there for your guest. And ideally this all leads to conversations on social media, people talking about your show, and hopefully even a retweet or comment from the guest on their social media pages.

Here's an example of a guest (Ross Simmonds) coming on my podcast and helping me to promote the episode afterward to his audience of 35,000 followers on Twitter:

 **Ross Simmonds** ✔
@TheCoolestCool
···

What's the future of B2B marketing?

👉 Brand evangelism
👉 More inspo from B2C
👉 More intentional distribution
👉 Long term content investments

@davegerhardt **and I discuss all of this and more in this
episode** 🔥🎧🔥

 Ross Simmonds on B2B Content, Influencer Marketing, & S...
Listen to this episode from The DGMG Podcast on Spotify.
Ross Simmonds (@thecoolestcool) is the Founder & CEO of...
🔗 open.spotify.com

4:31 PM · Mar 3, 2021 · Twitter for iPhone

In some cases, there's even an opportunity for cross-promotion. Your guest can go on your podcast, and you can go on theirs, and the cross-promotion between the shows will increase your reach. But like anything in marketing, this will only work if done in an organic way. No one wants a forty-five-minute advertisement disguised as a podcast interview. If you can find natural ways to promote each other's show, that works best.

Post-release of a guest on each episode, again, blanket your social media accounts. Create special graphics, video, audio, and written posts that can be shared with your guest. Share them on your accounts and ask the guest to do the same (most times they won't, and that's OK; sometimes they will, and when they do it's always worth it, so my advice is to over-prepare and offer up promo images people can share). You increase the chances of a guest sharing the episode by making sure the experience is a special one for them. For example, make a custom graphic of the two of you or your logos, and share it out on social media. Find ways to share their information with yours, and you will benefit from connecting with their audience. Create clips that make them look great or share something unique. We're all people, and the more you can make your podcast guest look good, the more likely they will be to share it with their audience too. *Yes. It's a bit vain. But it works. And this is a book about marketing and promoting your business. We should have crossed that bridge a while ago* ☺.

See how much content you can get from a single episode? This is why I love podcasting. But there's more. You can use the leverage from your podcast to extend your audience as a whole. You can use this content for *all* of your marketing. This is the real ROI on a podcast for me; this is the Trojan horse. It's not about the downloads. It's about using the podcast to:

- Create social content to build your audience on social media. For example, a tweet that hints at the top ten tips you will share in your next episode. But also: don't even promote the podcast; just use the content from the podcast to put out useful and relevant content about your niche to your dream customers. Do this consistently over time with the goal of building an audience as an expert in your niche. That is the ultimate goal. Just blasting out promotions for your podcast will not build you an audience, I promise. You have to add value in order to get value back (people following you, listening to your podcast).

- Build traffic to your website, blog, or membership site by taking the transcriptions of the podcast and turning them into articles, lists, and takeaways. You don't just have to write a post about the podcast episode—you can use the topics covered in the episode as evergreen content. For example: if I do an interview with a top CMO about her tips for hiring a marketing team, I can then go and write an article for my site about "How to Hire a World-Class Marketing Team" and use the content from my podcast episode as the source and inspiration. I usually recommend creating two articles from each podcast episode. First, a promo-style post, which recaps the episode and includes the full transcript and any show notes or links; and second, an "evergreen"-style post, which is more about longer tail traffic and hijacking one of the topics from your podcast episode to turn into a useful post for your website visitors in a way that almost has nothing to do with the fact that you have a podcast—the podcast is secondary. Here this article might only reference the podcast at the end: "PS, if you liked this topic, you'll love this interview with XYZ; click here to listen to the full episode."

- The podcast audio also makes for a ghostwriting gold mine. Think about it. It is a rich source of information, wording, and cadence for a ghostwriter who is writing for the founder or for the brand. For example, perhaps you, the founder, want to write a book about how you started your company. Your ghostwriter can go back and listen to the podcasts or read the transcripts and get verbatim wording on content, and they also can learn how you express yourself. As a marketer, I've struggled working with ghostwriters who are not able to match the tone and style of a founder or an exec, but the podcast provides almost a cheat code to nail the tone and style. A hundred episodes of the *Seeking Wisdom* podcast at Drift created hours of content from Drift founder David Cancel. As a founder and CEO, sitting down to write was not his thing, so we often relied on ghostwriters to write on his behalf. Using the podcast audio made this easy (trying to ghostwrite for an exec any other way is like pulling teeth). This alone is worth every dollar in podcast ROI.

- Build your email list through offering specials to listeners if they subscribe. Tim Ferriss does a nice job with this. He uses his popular podcast to plug his email list called "5-Bullet Friday" and records basically an "ad" for himself telling listeners to subscribe to his email list on his website. This is a great way to build an email list and truly own the audience from your podcast. You don't get any information about podcast listeners from Apple or Spotify (other than anonymous demographic information and what type of device they are listening on), so building your email list is essential for any podcast host. Another great way to build your email list is to offer something exclusive for email subscribers. For example, do a ten-minute exclusive interview with your podcast guest about a different topic that is only available to email subscribers (and when they join your list, you send them that interview). You can do this with any type of "bonus content" by offering listeners guides, templates, examples, tips, and more when they join your email list. You can also use this strategy to build a community. Facebook groups for podcast listeners/fans of the show work very well too. Social media is a good way to judge if your podcast would be a good fit to have an accompanying Facebook group. If you're getting tweets, comments, and emails about the show regularly, that's a good sign there's an engaged audience there. Building a place for the community to connect with each other can be a powerful way to add value and continue to build your audience. The Facebook group will work best if it's not just promoting new episodes of the show but is truly a place for like-minded people to start conversations related to your niche. For example, a podcast about sneakers would work well with a private Facebook group about sneakers. Or a podcast about chief financial officers would go well with a Facebook group for chief financial officers to connect with each other, talk privately, and share learnings with peers online. Create an event by using the best guests on the show as speakers at the event. Your listeners will already be familiar with them and will be hungry to learn more from them.

Many companies use events to build their brand and connect with customers. Let's say you've done a year of your podcast and put out a new show every week for fifty weeks. That's fifty episodes. These are conversations about topics that your niche, your dream customers, care about. As you're starting to think about the content and programming for your event, there's no better place to look than your podcast. Find the five to ten most popular episodes and use them as a jumping-off point to develop the talk tracks for the event. You've basically already just tested this content over the last year and proven that people want it (and there's no one more likely to attend your event than a regular podcast listener). Plus, if you've done interviews and had guests on the podcast, you can do the same thing: go back to your most popular guests and invite them to speak at your event.

- Write a book about your best podcast episodes or best podcast guests. You can bottle up everything I just mentioned about ghostwriting and an event and combine that advice and do the same thing with a book. Get a ghostwriter. Give them fifty episodes of content. Have them turn it into a book targeted at your dream customers in your niche (and because you've been podcasting and on social media for a year now, you'll have a good sense for what content resonates with people or not). At Privy, we used podcast interviews from our *Ecommerce Marketing School* podcast and turned them into expert lessons for our book and basically "crowdsourced" the content of a book about e-commerce marketing directly from our podcast. That book sold thousands of copies, and it was because we knew what content would land with our audience in book form because we had been podcasting and on social media for a year leading up to publication. See why there's so much ROI in podcasting?

- Hit the road and go on other podcasts, connecting with their audiences. As you refine your public speaking skills (and podcasting is a great way to do that) and your show grows, you'll hopefully start to get more requests from *other* podcast hosts to go on their shows. If you are in the first few years of focusing on building your brand as a founder with your podcast and social media, you should say yes to *every* podcast interview you can no matter how big or small, as long as the podcast is in your niche and your dream customers are listening. Part of this is about extending the reach of your show by going on other shows, of course ("Hey I liked her; I wonder if she has a podcast" is the reaction you're trying to get from listeners on other shows), but it's also about continuing to find your voice and hone your story. The best place to work on that is when someone else is interviewing you.

While building your podcast, you should also be going out and doing mini public relations tours. I recommend doing them once a quarter if you can. Make a list (or have the marketing team to do this) of podcasts you want to be on, events where you want to speak, and awards you'd want to win, and work to be at those events. If you are a founder of a very small company without staffing to search out these opportunities for you, you will need to do the legwork, but you're usually right in the middle of these conversations online and probably already going to some of these events today. However, if you have them, members of your team can do the research and some of the contacting for you to find these opportunities. Being a podcast host can be an incredible way to improve your skills as a public speaker. Most events will want to hear you talk before they'd ask you to present in front of their audience, and there's no better way to "show your work" than by having a podcast. It can be a great gateway to more public speaking opportunities.

Targeting other guests for your show can also do this too: for example, at Privy we put the experts in our book— they were all taking pictures, sharing it out, emailing their lists. That leads to more people finding us. More people bought the book. More people listened to our podcast. That's the power of tapping into other people's audiences in addition to your own—as your network grows, your audience grows too.

A final trick is to use the concept of *surprise and delight* to create superfans. Reach out to followers and give them a little gift. Create a logo for your podcast and send stickers out to a small group of followers. Write a book, send a copy to a few. Give shoutouts to followers. Send Starbucks gift cards. Show you care. A budget of $100 a month could go a long way to engage some superfans. And those superfans will work as your biggest advocates in telling other people about the show. If you have superfans, find a way to reward them. If you've been on the other end, you know it always feels good to get something from a show or person you enjoy following. You have the opportunity to create that feeling on your own with very little effort. And those super-fans often stick around forever. I can think of a few people individually who became fans of *Seeking Wisdom* at Drift and have since followed me and supported me in whatever I've done (*Henry J. and Robert G., if you're reading this, what's up?*).

HOW DO YOU KNOW IF IT'S WORKING?

While we will talk about feedback and metrics more fully in a later chapter, if you have started a podcast, you want to know if it is working. Metrics and engagement are the keys to knowing if your podcast is working. Are you getting downloads (you'll see these metrics from Transistor, Libsyn, or wherever you decide to host your podcast)? Are they increasing over time? Is it getting mentioned on other platforms by your audience? What do the reviews say? How long will it take to see if it is working?

Erik Jacobson of Lemonpie also stresses the importance of taking *time* to see if your podcast is gaining traction: "Most of the value you're going to capture from your show will be from doing it for six plus months. Most podcasters quit too early."

Six months. It sounds like forever, but it really isn't that long. When you start a podcast, I recommend planning to do it for at least twelve months. At the six-month marker, you should be able to see the growth. If not, think about what the engagement of your audience is saying to you in regards to what needs to change. Is it the length? Frequency? Format? Is it showing you both being a creator and doing your work in public? What are the comments telling you? Suck it up, read the comments, and learn from them.

Plan your podcast well, do it consistently for more than six months, and then you will see the metrics showing you the growth of your audience.

The goal of launching your podcast is to become the number one resource in your particular industry. This won't happen overnight, but with consistency and a clear plan, it will happen.

When you begin, your audience will be small. That's OK; it will grow, and those early shows and listeners can give you feedback on how to improve.

BUT I REALLY DON'T WANT TO DO THIS...

I have talked with founders who hate the sound of their own voice in recordings or recording videos. They use these excuses to justify why a podcast is a bad fit.

The video is somewhat optional. Talking is not—how can you have a podcast without talking? But in all seriousness: you're already doing this! Any founder has talked about their business a lot. For hours, days, even months. They have talked to investors, potential customers, competitors, family and friends, and probably the family dog. All I'm asking you to do now is record some of these conversations (and you can even leave out the sensitive information, so there's no risk here).

These should be conversations that are already happening. I just want you to leave this book with your brain turned on to what interesting topics could be. When you're thinking about what episodes to record next, think about the interesting meetings and conversations you've had lately. In most cases, the content for your next podcast episode is right there. Now you just need to go tell it to the microphone.

By the way: swallow your own nerves about how your voice sounds. Who cares? We all think our voices sound funny when we hear them back. Instead, recognize this is the best possible avenue for sharing your expertise with the world and know that it will be worth it regardless of how many people listen (remember: the podcast is the Trojan horse anyway). Side note: it gets easier the more you do it, and over time, you no longer will think about how your voice sounds, I promise.

WAYS TO GUARANTEE SUCCESS

As you start your podcast, here are some tips for increasing the chances of success:

- For at least your first episodes, over-prepare. Have notes, funny quotes, and statistics. Admit you are nervous, make it part of the show, and go forward. When I first began my podcast, I over-prepared because sometimes the guest on the other end wasn't as willing to chat off the cuff as I was, so having notes and prep made each episode fail proof. I always had enough content to keep an interview going even if there wasn't much of a two-way conversation. But now having done hundreds of episodes, I am comfortable in almost any scenario with any guest, so I don't prepare (I also know the topics and know the content my audience wants, so I am comfortable going into each interview without a plan).

- Being an expert in your industry is great. Being obnoxious as to how knowledgeable you are will turn people off. The goal is not to tell people you're an expert. Show them with a great podcast that makes them smarter, better, stronger, whatever you want to achieve. It's not about you, it's about your audience. Lead with value.

- Be interesting. This is not the dull lecture about ROI that you endured during your MBA training. Make it interesting and relatable. A podcast is great because it can be you—not something ghostwritten. It's actually you. So try to be you on the mic. Think of your favorite podcast hosts. Do you love them because of how formal and buttoned up they are? My guess is no. This doesn't mean you have to do things out of a character, but just be you. The best podcasts are conversational.

- Show your process. Talk about what you did to prepare. Talk about what this podcast means to you. Talk a bit about your brand. This doesn't have to be over-scripted. Podcasting is about being real, authentic, and human.

- Give a teaser of the upcoming (the next) episode or episodes. This means you need to be planning in advance. The best way to promote future episodes of your podcast is right now, on your podcast. Talk about upcoming guests and future ideas.

- Ask for reviews and feedback. I like to do this at the end of each episode. Ratings and reviews do help drive rankings on platforms like Apple Podcasts, which helps more people find your show. So I usually spend a quick minute at the end of each episode asking people to leave a review if they are enjoying the show, and I also ask for people to tweet at me to send me questions, give feedback, or just connect about the show.

- *Related to this:* one of the best ways to get additional guests for your podcast is to ask each guest (after the interview) to recommend one other person to come on your podcast. I've found that not only do most people recommend someone good, but they also offer to make the introduction for you (assuming the interview went well, of course, and they enjoyed doing it). Now you just got a new guest recommendation and an intro from a relevant source.

YOUR TURN

You are going to start a podcast, but to do so, you need to make some decisions.

1. Do research. Look into podcasts that may be targeting the same niche. Listen to them. What do you like about them? Dislike? How can you make yourself stand out from the crowd? Go back to role models. Who is your role model for your podcast? Go and make your version of that show and *then* innovate and make it yours. Copy what works and innovate.

2. When you think about your niche, how can you make sure that your format and content will resonate with them?

3. Decide on format. Will it be just you talking, sharing your expertise and your process? Will you do interviews? Or will you just tell customers' stories?

4. How long will each episode be?

5. Get the needed equipment, and line up the services you need, such as the editor.

6. How often can you commit to doing an episode? You should release an episode at least once a week. Be realistic in your expectations of yourself.

7. Are you going to do an off-the-cuff podcast of you just talking, or are you more of a write-a-script person? Know yourself, and make sure you are comfortable with the format.

8. How long of a podcast do you want to have? Some podcasters do mini-podcasts, under thirty minutes. Others consistently do an hour or more. Decide on how long you want each episode to be.

9. Set a schedule for recording episodes. Before you launch your podcast, you should have at least six episodes ready to go so that you can release them on schedule while you continue to make more.

10. Post teasers of upcoming episodes, share them again and again, and look for ways to reward superfans.

11. Now may be the time to double-check how you reward your superfans. Special knowledge? Backstage access? Early-bird access? Gifts? Have you done anything?

12. Pay attention to the feedback! Did listeners comment that they wished the episode was longer? Shorter? Respond, and then adjust if it feels right. Are there guests they want to hear? Topics they want you to cover that you haven't? Ideas on how you can grow the show? This is why I love connecting podcasting and social media. The feedback loop allows you to tap into the wisdom of the crowd (and here, the wisdom is from not just the crowd but your niche, your dream customers).

Podcasting is the start to becoming a publisher and thinking like a media company, not just a founder. But starting a podcast is not some magic trick that will automatically work to build your brand as a founder and put your business on the map. Once you launch your podcast, then you need to get ready to go out into the world, hit the road, and share your message in other ways.

CHAPTER 8

HIT THE ROAD

O ne of my favorite quotes about the need to hit the road is from Ted Turner: "Early to bed, early to rise, work like hell, and advertise."

This is the motto you must take with your business if you want to be successful. My point is this: you must assume that people will not come to you. It's not enough to become a storyteller. You must be proactive about getting out there and telling that story to the world.

When I teach classes on this topic, I tell my students that I believe that 99.9 percent of founders will need to hit the road to grow their audience. The audience is out *there* and needs you to come to them. I know, that sounds counterintuitive after all the discussion of social media and podcasting, but it isn't. The most overused quote in marketing comes from the movie *Field of Dreams* but with the opposite strategy: just because you built it doesn't mean that people will come. You must go out and tell them to come.

You must become a great public spokesperson for your brand. You know more about your brand than anyone else and are the best, sometimes the only, person who can share your brand with the world. Once you are out there, you'll quickly see there is no better feedback loop than public speaking.

Just as you have prioritized your use of social media and your podcast, you also need to prioritize public speaking. This isn't new for founders; think of the interviews with Steve Jobs at All Things Digital, or Marc Benioff on CNBC, Harley Finkelstein on Squawk Box, and even Elon Musk on Saturday Night Live. Think about the TED Talks you've devoured, learning about founders.

What I love about marketing and brand building today in 2021 and beyond is that unlike those folks, you don't need to be a billionaire founder on a mainstream media channel to get your message out to the world (because here you're becoming your own publisher), but you still must embrace getting out there just like those founders did. If you can get comfortable being "a promoter," you'll be able to tap into bigger audiences to spread your message. Personally, I think every founder should be on a constant "book tour" for their company.

How do you do this? Accept every speaking opportunity you get in the first two years of building your brand. I suggest speaking at every event and going on every podcast that you can manage in your schedule, no matter how small. This is about finding your voice. You need to be ready to speak in front of a bigger crowd. Most founders I talk to want to speak in front of large crowds but haven't yet told their story to a group of twenty strangers.

Go back to the 1980s and '90s in Vermont, prior to the advent of social media. Ben & Jerry's ice cream was known statewide. Every Vermont kid knew the story of how they had started the company in an old gas station garage in Burlington, Vermont. As the business grew, they offered Vermont schools free ice cream for events if, well, it got mentioned in some way. They offered to speak at events as well. High schools took them up on their generosity, and they supplied decadent, frozen dairy treats for multitudes of high school students and talked to thousands of students over the years. The trade-off for their generosity? Every local paper carried stories that noted the donation, and those stories were shared out nationally. But today, you can do all this on your own without relying on the media. Bring a video camera, or an intern with a video camera, or your video team (there are varying levels of readers and budgets for this book, so I used all those examples, I know). Leverage that video content for social media. Pull out quotes and clips. Take the audio from the event, record an intro, and then run it as an episode of your podcast. Heck, maybe there are two podcast episodes in there because there was Q&A after your talk, and you can run that as a separate segment. And at the very least, you can have the video to watch back and learn from after. You can't master your story if you don't practice your story. That is what this is about. Any audience that's there is a bonus. But that's the goal. Over time, an invitation to speak at an event with twenty people can become an invite to an event with two hundred (that's happened to me; speaking at a small event, you never know who's in the audience; a woman came up to me and commented that I was a good speaker and she was programming content for an event in San Diego—the following year I was speaking in front of two hundred people).

FIND YOUR VOICE

As mentioned in the previous chapter, you can also hit the virtual road as a guest on other podcasts. I count that as speaking too, and for most people, it will be more likely that you'll be able to be a guest on someone's podcast vs. speaking at their event (no disrespect to you at all; it's literally easier to do a podcast than an event, so why not focus there too?). Think about it like this: if you did one guest podcast once a week, you would have appeared on fifty-two of them in a year, bringing your message to a whole new audience. You won't do fifty-two interviews, but c'mon, you can do five or ten or twenty. These are all important to expand your audience, yes, but ultimately, in the early days, this is not about promotion, it's about finding your voice. You need to be out there at least a few times per month. Be interesting and be everywhere. The more you build up your brand and your social media presence, the more inbound opportunities you will get. At Drift, I booked David Cancel on as many as I could possibly squeeze into his schedule so we could keep refining our message. And with our own podcast cranking weekly plus his activity on social media, there were endless topics and opportunities for him to discuss on other people's podcasts or at their events.

Regardless of where you start, always niche down. Start with a few smaller podcasts that you might be able to get on pretty easily, and build from there. As part of this process, you need to find your voice and build your credibility. So, in the beginning, say yes to everything. Get as many reps going on other people's podcasts as you can, and then in the future, you're doing outreach and someone has already heard of you, because they've seen you on three, four, or five other industry podcasts. By starting small, you can find success and then grow accordingly.

Some will go well. Some will be awful. Some will be train wrecks that you will cringe about when you remember them. Make sure you always get a copy of the recording and listen to it and reflect on it. It is better to stink on a small podcast while you are refining your message than to smell up the room in front of an international audience when being interviewed on CNBC, right?

Think of it as a training ground, not promotion. This is for you, not for the world, but as you get better, the benefits change.

As you improve, the goal becomes getting your name out there, cross-promoting your podcast—since I am assuming you now have one—and making yourself and your brand thought leaders in the eyes and ears of the viewing and listening public.

SHARE YOUR STORY, ADD VALUE, AND MAKE CONNECTIONS

You have to do your research and find the podcasts that have an engaged audience that will be receptive to you and your brand. Look around your existing network of customers, investors, advisors, and companies in your niche. With over a million podcasts in rotation on Apple Podcasts and Spotify today, you know someone in your niche with a podcast you could probably get on. But why should they have you on? You have something new and different to offer to that audience that the host can't provide themself. You can't just come on hoping to drop a plug without giving some value in return. The best podcast interviews are not promotions. They are not advertisements. They are genuine conversations between two experts in a niche. Do your homework and come with a pitch—what can you bring to the table? Not about you, not about your company, but *for* the audience.

As you try to make connections with podcast hosts, get creative in your outreach. Podcast hosts aren't hiding; they're everywhere online. Most people with a podcast are active on social media, and you can reach them there. Or, track down their email and contact them personally; a clear, concise, interesting email, stating why you are a great fit for that podcast will help.

But remember, they get a lot of requests, so they probably don't have much time to stroll leisurely through their inboxes. This means that you need to do something that stands out to get their attention, such as write some witty copy or record a personal video pitch. Or even do something to indirectly get their attention. For example, maybe you had a recent marketing video go viral or a super well-known e-book. Preface your outreach by saying you're the mind behind some cool marketing thing, and you'd love to come and discuss the creation process. If you have something people want to hear about, use it. And don't be afraid to just shoot your shot. Shoot 'em a DM and see what happens. I once cold emailed a reporter from the *New York Times* on a Sunday evening with a pitch to do an interview with David Cancel at Drift. The pitch (if I admit now) wasn't spectacular, but I happened to send him a message at a random time when he was checking email. I got him to respond to my email, and we started a conversation that led to an interview in NYC two months later.

My advice here is not to lead with a gimmick, but if you're an expert in a niche, your unique perspective can be valuable for someone else's audience. Always make it about their podcast and their listeners, not you. As a podcast host myself, I love having guests that I know my audience wants to hear from because this improves the quality of my show and positions me as a trust expert in my niche.

Think about their audience first, and then how you can add value for the listeners.

With any outreach, my goal is to start a conversation. I don't try to stuff a thousand words into an email. I try to get a response from a relevant person and start a conversation and *then* lay down the pitch. Focus on starting conversations and getting replies vs. blasting out random pitches.

When you're looking for places to land, don't overlook your network. Look for connections you share with the host of the podcast you'd like to pitch. Is there anyone that has a sliver of a connection to you? If so, use it.

You also need to create a newsworthy hook that you'll pitch to them. Maybe you have a new book out, a big product launch, or big company news. The hook provides context and relevance to your pitch. The goal, however, is not to come on the podcast and exclusively talk about that thing—no one wants a podcast guest to come on and just pitch their thing. Find a way to connect it back to the benefit of that podcast audience. You've seen this a million times with celebrities doing book tours. The hook, the reason they are doing a bunch of press or podcast interviews, is because they have a new book out. But they don't spend the whole hour plugging the book.

If you are cringing at the thought of how much time this outreach will take, that is normal. It will take time. If that time is a problem for you, have someone in your organization do the research and connections for you. For example, David Cancel wasn't emailing podcasters to pitch himself; I was doing that for him. That's where the marketing team comes into play. Plus there are many agencies that you can hire to help you find potential podcasts; for example, Lemonpie is a great one that can arrange a personalized and highly targeted podcast tour based upon your goals, your niche, and your product. For some founders, paying an agency to do the legwork is a great investment. But also remember that you're the founder. You're probably connected to a few of these people already, and often getting on someone else's show can be as easy as sending a DM on Twitter.

YOUR TURN

Start small and make a list of five podcasts you would like to do a guest appearance on, and reach out to them to offer yourself for an interview. Don't pick the biggest podcasts in the world, please. Pick five you think you can actually get on (OK, four and one stretch is fine too).

After those five, make a list of ten more, and send out requests in batches of five. I always recommend doing this vs. blasting out pitches, because you don't want to burn through them all with a pitch that isn't landing. Send out five. See if people respond or not. Tweak the message with what you learned. Try five more.

The next step is to search out public speaking opportunities.

List ten events coming in the next six months that you are likely to attend. Reach out to see if you can join a panel presentation, keynote, or fireside chat. Take the same approach as above with staggering your pitches to get feedback and adjust. If there are no speaking opportunities available or they don't accept you, no sweat. A reputation as a speaker takes time to build and there's no guarantee (even as a great speaker) that someone will accept you. Instead, attend the event and reach out to speakers on the agenda and offer to interview them on-site for your podcast during the event. This is one of the best ways to

(1) get content from an event, (2) connect with industry influencers, and (3) tap into the event and "hijack" it for the benefit of your podcast. In 2019 after submitting to speak at SaaStr Annual and getting rejected, we did exactly this at Drift. The result was five podcast episodes with big-name guests in our industry (everyone said yes because they were already there on-site at the event, so the barrier to record was very low). We ended up turning those episodes into podcasts that reached 10,000 people via our blog and podcast feed—and I'm not sure speaking at the event would have done even close to that ☺.

LEVEL

3

CHAPTER 9

BECOME A MASTER OF THE FEEDBACK LOOP

You are the founder. Your story and explainer are captivating. Your podcast is gaining followers, and your social media accounts are bringing you new followers daily. You've taken your show on the road, joining others on their podcasts and speaking at events. And if you've taken those things from this book so far, you're already making more progress than 99 percent of founders out there. No, I can't cite a source on that stat. Actually, yes, I can: the source is me, and I know that nine out of ten founders will think or talk about becoming better at storytelling, launching a podcast, or being active on social media—and maybe even read this book—but never make the time to actually do it. If you become active on those channels and launch a podcast, you're already doing more than most.

But here's where this thing goes from Level 2 to Level 3: the feedback loop.

Now it's time to understand the power of having an audience (yes, even a small one) and using their feedback to influence what you create with the future, and to see how it's almost a cheat code for ensuring the success of what you're putting out into the world.

One of the most powerful things in business and marketing today is the ability to get feedback directly from your dream customers without having to spend a dollar to earn their attention. Plus this feedback happens in real time via social media, so you can get a gut check on something almost instantly. If you can learn to master this feedback loop, you will have unlocked the whole game with content, social media, and podcasting.

A quick personal story: Now that I've been doing this for the last ten years online in the marketing niche, I feel like I should never put out something people are not interested in. Because of my audience on social media, I can get feedback on nearly any idea and use that feedback before even launching something. I can also use that feedback to guide what things I should create in the future and almost "foolproof" their success. If hundreds of people on LinkedIn told me they would find value in a book about how to build a brand for a startup founder, I would feel pretty good about going to create that book, because I know there's at least an initial audience there. In fact, that's exactly how I developed the idea for this book, and I've been using my private Facebook group, DGMG, to test book ideas with 2,500+ members.

I've even created a few mini-contests to help build up hype for the book and to get genuine feedback from a group of people who are most likely to buy my book.

And the result is not just online. I have primed my audience for the book and hopefully gotten them excited about buying it, but as I'm writing this book, I have a good feeling about launching the book, because I've already tested the concept with the DGMG community. And this example is not specific to a Facebook group. These types of posts will work anywhere you have an audience online. I could have also posted these questions to my LinkedIn followers and Twitter followers, but early on in the life of the book,

Dave Gerhardt

Admin · April 12 · 🌐

Hey. Can you help me with my book title?

Comment with your best titles by Wednesday.

And I'll pick one winner and send that new Shure MV7 mic 😊

The book is about the power of the Founder/CEO brand -- and how to build it through storytelling, social media, and podcasting.

I believe that most marketing teams should be focusing on *also* marketing the founder's brand, in addition to simply telling the company/product story.

Build a brand for the founder can be a huge advantage, but I haven't seen anyone write about how to do it -- so I thought I'd share my lessons / framework for the first time.

The book will include lessons from Drift -- we interviewed David Cancel for the book. And Hiten Shah. It will include lessons from Privy -- we interviewed Ben Jabbawy. And also experts from like Ross Simmonds and Erik Bison Jacobson on content and podcasting.

Anyway, I can't give away much more right now but I need to deliver the title this week! So I thought I'd turn to DGMG.

Founder Brand
How to Use Storytelling, Social Media, & Podcasting to Build an Audience That Will Buy From Your Business

🏷 Attached topics #FounderBrand

👍❤ 17   86 Comments

I wanted to keep the idea private and only for my group members. But I do something similar often with Twitter and LinkedIn. For example, I had an idea to start a marketing breakfast in the Boston startup community, but I didn't want to invest in the event unless I knew people were interested in it. Because I have an audience of marketers (at the time in Boston) who follow my content on Twitter and LinkedIn, I got to test the idea before investing in it. In the example on the following page, I even created an email alias and asked people to email me if they wanted to come.

As a result of this tweet, I had fifty to one hundred emails in my inbox from people telling me that if I hosted a breakfast they would come. I felt pretty good about going to invest in an event and that people would actually show up because of it—and even had emails from companies asking to sponsor and offering up venues to host and pay for the food. When I think about social media and going beyond vanity metrics, this is the type of stuff I'm talking about. There is huge value in having an audience of followers in your niche. And it's never too late to start.

Dave Gerhardt
@davegerhardt

···

🏭Attention Boston Marketers 🏭

I'm starting a quarterly breakfast for marketers in Boston in January.

2:22 PM · Dec 8, 2019 · Twitter Web App

᛫᛫᛫ View Tweet activity

5 Retweets   **2** Quote Tweets   **52** Likes

♡   ⟲   ♡   ⬆

Dave Gerhardt @davegerhardt · Dec 8, 2019   ···
Replying to @davegerhardt
I hate networking events, but I think there's an opportunity for a regular breakfast with 10-20-30-100 (hopefully) of the best marketers here in Boston.

*And uh, well -- selfishly, this will help me with recruiting since I can't hire any marketers from Drift 😅😅😅

♡ 2   ⟲   ♡ 5   ⬆   ᛫᛫᛫

Dave Gerhardt @davegerhardt · Dec 8, 2019   ···
(In all seriousness, events like these can be GREAT if the right people show up, and I'm hoping to help make that happen and then do it quarterly).

I will post more details in the next few weeks.

♡ 1   ⟲   ♡   ⬆   ᛫᛫᛫

Dave Gerhardt @davegerhardt · Dec 8, 2019   ···
>>> Send an email to dgmarketingbreakfast[at]gmail and I will send you an email when I have the date/time/location.

Or tag someone in this tweetstorm thing or send them this link. See ya.

♡ 1   ⟲   ♡ 5   ⬆   ᛫᛫᛫

Dave Gerhardt @davegerhardt · Dec 8, 2019   ···
If you're a local CMO / VP of Marketing: I'm happy to get you involved too if you want to buy coffee, etc. I'm sure we can work out some type of lead share 🙂

♡ 1   ⟲   ♡ 7   ⬆   ᛫᛫᛫

MASTER OF THE FEEDBACK LOOP: THE REAL
ROI OF YOUR BECOMING A PUBLISHER

This is the secret power of this whole playbook. It's not just that you're on social media now and you have a podcast that you're publishing regularly. Now you have the assets you need to create more marketing (without spending time coming up with new content), to be everywhere and to create air cover for your brand. The combination of social media and podcasting can transform you from a founder to a mini media company. No more waiting around for the press to write about you to get people in your industry to start talking about your business. Use feedback from your audience to drive content ideas and product ideas.

Now we'll talk about how to use this leverage to build an audience and in return build your brand.

For years I thought that the ROI of doing a podcast was how big the audience got. As a result, I focused on always trying to find little ways to optimize and grow my podcast audience. But that thinking about the ROI was wrong. The real ROI of creating a podcast today is that it can be a Trojan horse for all of your marketing content. When I say that your podcast is a Trojan horse, it is because audio gives you the ultimate leverage.

One of the best marketing channels a business can have is through the voice of the founder. People (your customers) want to feel like they are working with experts. The founder is usually the one who *is* the expert in the industry. So it would be a great strategy to have that founder regularly sharing ideas and putting "thought leadership" out into the market, whether that's via social media, blogging, writing a newsletter, contributing op-eds and guest articles, or speaking at industry events.

But as anyone who's ever tried to "get content" from a founder can tell you, it's nearly impossible. Founders are busy. They are in everything: sales, marketing, recruiting, financing, partnerships. And so despite the marketing team's dreams, it's often impossible to get that founder to sit down to produce any of the thought leadership content I mentioned above.

A solution marketing teams and founders often turn to is a ghostwriter. And I tried to do this for the founder at Drift. I was the marketing person trying to create thought leadership content for the founder (David Cancel). But I couldn't find a writer who could match David's style and tone (and I know many marketers struggle with the same thing).

But that's exactly where our podcast *Seeking Wisdom* gave us so much leverage. After a few weeks of trying, I decided to ditch the ghostwriting efforts and do it myself. But I had a secret weapon: our podcast. I started ghost-writing for David, and I didn't have to (a) try to imitate his style and tone, or (b) try to find more time on his already busy calendar to interview him for ghostwritten content. I had our podcast. I would sit and listen to a podcast episode for thirty minutes, build an outline of the article I wanted to write, and then go line by line and write down how David said it on the podcast. The result was near perfect ghostwriting—because it wasn't even ghostwriting. I was using the words he actually said! I was just the one typing them into blog posts, articles, and newsletters.

Over time, this format gave us a ton of leverage because I was able to use conversations with David and steer him into all sorts of directions depending on what content we needed. If we wanted to have a great article written by the

CEO for our next product launch, well, I'd just interview him directly—and we'd publish it on our podcast so the audience could get some benefit too. It was like a two for one (at least) with every podcast interview.

And the reach of the podcast went beyond just the founder brand and David's social media channels. Our podcast at Drift helped inspire messaging for the company's social media channels, website, emails, and more. *Seeking Wisdom* became the jumping-off point for teams across the company to listen and take the founder's words and sprinkle them into what they were working on. The podcast was an anchor for all of our marketing efforts. If we were doing an event, we'd be talking about it on our podcast. If we were hosting a dinner in a local town with customers, we'd be talking about it on our podcast. All of this helped us create leverage with content, but it also allowed us to create our own mini publishing company in our niche. Yes, press is nice to get. But with Drift we didn't have to *wait* for the press to write about us to reach our customers. We were doing it with an audience that we built on our own. And when you create a direct relationship with your audience through content like this, you also get the benefit of a feedback loop. You're getting likes, comments, shares, retweets, and direct messages about the ideas you're putting out into the world in real time. Yes, likes and retweets do not always directly correlate to revenue, but they serve as a great proxy for understanding what people might be interested in.

This feedback can also flow in the opposite direction. A tweet that got reactions could lead to a blog post and, in turn, become the basis of a podcast episode. We also used responses to our podcasts and posts to determine what events to host, who to invite to speak, and what to create in the future.

On a smaller scale, just to give you an idea of how this can work, I put out this tweet that said "busy is not a flex"— meaning that the end goal is not to be busy. There are no trophies for how busy you are (although at work sometimes it can feel like that one guy on the team is in a meeting competition). In fact (at least for me anyway), I want to measure my success by how not busy I am. Like I am so not busy, me and the family are in Hawaii for three months, not busy.

Anyway, I tweeted this line—and instantly it started getting comments like "this should be a T-shirt!"

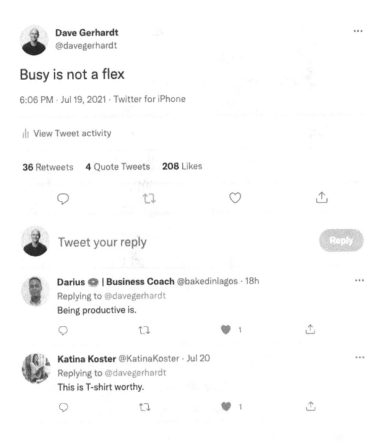

Dave Gerhardt
@davegerhardt

Busy is not a flex

6:06 PM · Jul 19, 2021 · Twitter for iPhone

View Tweet activity

36 Retweets   **4** Quote Tweets   **208** Likes

Tweet your reply

Darius 🍩 | Business Coach @bakedinlagos · 18h
Replying to @davegerhardt
Being productive is.

Katina Koster @KatinaKoster · Jul 20
Replying to @davegerhardt
This is T-shirt worthy.

As of writing this book I haven't put it on a T-shirt, but I have a damn good feeling that if I *did* put it on a T-shirt, I could sell it. And because I've been putting out relevant content in my niche for a decade now (my niche is mostly startups, marketing), I have built up a following of relevant people in that niche. People follow like-minded people. I bet the audience buying this shirt would be a good match for my audience: people who work in marketing at startups are often obsessed with time management and productivity. I think this T-shirt would be a hit with them. OK, I'm rambling now, and you get the point. But this is important, and I don't want to let this example seem silly. Think about how powerful this could be for your business. What if you had a direct feedback loop with potential customers and didn't have to spend a dollar to get feedback on ideas from them? I have used my social media channels over and over again to my advantage this way, and you can 100 percent do this too if you're ready to commit to becoming a publisher.

To give another example, let's look at what I did at Privy. After joining as CMO and rebuilding the marketing team, we put this exact playbook into play. Our goal was to boost Privy's awareness and visibility in the market and to position the company as the *leader* in e-commerce marketing for *small businesses* (good example of a niche, by the way). I knew that to do this we'd need two things: (1) a lot of content, and (2) reach. And so the two channels we used were a podcast and the founder's social media presence (Ben Jabbawy is the founder/CEO at Privy, and he's on Twitter @jabbawy). To get this kick-started, I started off the show as host (to require even less time from the founder until we proved out the concept). The first thirty episodes of the podcast were interviews with industry experts, and they were a smash hit. Ben would tweet and share video clips from each episode on his social media channels, and this helped jumpstart his social media content production. He had been tweeting for years as a founder, but never as consistently as when he had fresh content coming regularly via the podcast every week. This helped continue to establish Ben as an authority on e-commerce marketing as the founder of Privy.

To leverage our efforts, we looked at our feedback, and we then took the top podcast episodes (most downloaded and the ones that felt like they had the most chatter on social media when the team would share them out) and invited those guests to host Privy "masterclasses," which were sixty-minute deep dives on a particular topic, and the Zoom calls were open to any Privy customer or podcast listener. And we'd even record those sessions and then publish them a few weeks later on our podcast. These were different from the interviews with the expert guest and instead were more like listeners observing a master-class at a whiteboard going deep on marketing strategies and tactics. This also helped us promote the podcast to our entire customer base. We were never promoting the podcast directly but always leading with the value and self-ish benefit to our customers: you can learn how to grow your business and all you have to do is pop in your AirPods and listen to our podcast while you're working out, com-muting to work, or doing chores around the house.

The Privy podcast worked as a Trojan horse for building up our blog. Each podcast episode could be transcribed via a service like Rev.com, edited by Lauren on the con-tent team, and turned into a blog post (and oftentimes we could get two or three articles from a single episode). The podcast worked as a Trojan horse for speaking word of mouth about Privy through our podcast. We'd arm each podcast guest with video clips of them speaking (and make them look amazing, of course), and they'd help pro-mote the episode by sharing the clip on their social media channels. None of these people would share our stuff if it was an ad or something overly promotional for Privy, but they would certainly share it if it was about them and also made them sound smart and look great in front of their customers (and this is why guests are one of the best ways to grow your podcast; in most cases guests will say yes to come on your podcast if they can make the dates work, and if they come on your podcast they will often like, comment, and share content from the episode they were on). And on top of that, because of the reach we had built up on social media through my account, the CEO's account (Ben Jabbawy's), and having the rest of the Privy team excited about sharing each episode (which happens when the content is not overly salesy and promotional but is more focused on lessons, learnings, expertise, and making potential customers smarter), we were able to be part of the discussion in the e-commerce marketing industry on social media and use those insights to fuel future episodes. Responses and discussions (even conversations we were not in but just observing by following industry influencers) could then help guide what episodes we should create in the future and give us a good sense of what our audience would be interested in before we actually went and created another episode. This is the value of the feed-back loop you create as a publisher. And speaking of the leverage you get from a podcast: here's an example. Before COVID-19 hit we even had plans for an in-person event with 500 customers, and the speakers and content for that event were going to be solely based on popular podcast episodes. Instead we turned many of the interviews from the podcast into a book. This wasn't an e-book or a PDF. This was a physical, printed book that we created, and the product was so good we were even able to sell the book. We didn't offer it for free. It was a real book that anyone could purchase from our store online:

The result of charging for the book was that we were basically able to build an incredible "lead magnet" for Privy, but instead of us having to find a way to get a marketing budget for this, the book paid for itself. And the people who would read this type of book would most likely be people who would be a good fit to use the Privy product. See how this can work? Again, the power of a niche. And why podcasting can be the Trojan horse for your marketing engine.

You have the niche. You have the leverage and reach through your podcast.

Now you have an audience. Learn through your audience. When you do that, all of the above examples are possible with your business and with your brand.

And this is why you can't just hire an intern to do your social media or build your podcast. This actually needs to be *you* if you want to reap the rewards from it.

Think of it another way. Let's say you have a restaurant, and everybody comes in and they ask for this type of sandwich or this particular thing that you don't make. Suddenly, you realize how many people are asking for it. You should go and create it and add it to the menu. Making a mention of "Due to customers' requests" will show your audience that you care about their feedback.

Sometimes you may want to seek feedback by asking direct questions. For example, "I'm thinking about writing a book. What should I write about?" That's how I got to this idea for the book.

You will begin to notice patterns and trends that you can use. If you can learn from the feedback and use it to inform your choices, you will have a huge advantage in creating what people want. That is the power of social media and a podcast and having an email list: the relationship with your audience is market research.

The real value of social media for a brand is not that it's a place to promote your stuff. It's a place to get feedback. Master the feedback loop.

I KNOW, YOU WANT METRICS TOO

OK, I hope you get the concept of the Trojan horse. The idea is one of the most powerful when it comes to content and brand building, and it's one of the reasons I always try to create an "anchor show" at every company I'm doing marketing for (Privy's *Ecommerce Marketing School*, Drift's *Seeking Wisdom*, and I even launched HubSpot's *Growth Show* podcast when I worked there). But if you're a founder or in marketing, I know you want more too, and you're not going to let me off the hook here without talking about metrics, so let's talk. For social media, when I think about metrics and feedback, I look at three buckets: followers, engagement, and inbounds. For podcasting, I look at two buckets: downloads and inbounds.

Followers

Followers is the most simple and straightforward of the three. Some marketing experts talk about followers in terms of it being a vanity metric, but at its heart, if you have more followers, it generally is because you are putting out interesting content consistently. Call it a vanity metric if you want, but I'm not sure anyone can argue that having more followers is a bad thing. Anyway, keep in mind two caveats when you think about the number of followers. First, your number of followers is not going to jump exponentially overnight. If it takes weeks or even months for your numbers to grow, don't worry. As of this writing,

I've been on Twitter for twelve years and just crossed 30,000 followers. I've been focusing on LinkedIn for three years and went from 10,000 followers to 100,000 over that short period (which was during a time LinkedIn's reach was exploding; I was there and able to ride the wave, but this happens on many social media channels, especially if you have the foresight to join early). The second caveat is that audience size is relative. You targeted a small niche, so it is likely that your number of followers will be small in the beginning. And honestly, depending on your niche, the size might not matter.

Engagement

Engagement is the second part of metrics as you look at your social media presence. Those stratospheric follower numbers don't mean anything if they are not picking up what you're putting down. And the best benchmark for that with social media is *engagement*. If you have 10,000 Twitter followers, but not a single person comments on your tweet about your brand or a new idea, I would say you don't have a list of dream customers following you, you have bots, fake followers, or people who are just looking for followers themselves. To give a specific example, I recently worked with a CEO who is consistently putting content out on social media. However, it wasn't catching the attention of the audience, so one tweet might have a few likes, but no comments, no real engagement. Now, as we have tweaked the content to make it more relevant to the founder brand, as well as make it more interesting and authentic, the comments are pouring in, which is true engagement. Unfortunately, there is no simple metric across both Twitter and LinkedIn. Twitter gives you some useful stats under *analytics.twitter.com* but no engagement rate, and LinkedIn shares the engagement rate (the number of reactions, comments, and shares compared to the number of people who saw the post) only for company pages, not personal profiles. So—and the analytics crowd is not going to love this one, but here goes—I just use my gut. You will know when more people start responding. How many people comment on your stuff today? One? None? Three people all from your company? Whatever it is, use that as a benchmark. And over time, if you're putting out relevant, useful content for a specific niche, you will start to get more responses. This is yet another reason why you have to actually be there using social media for yourself. It's the only way to know what's working, because what's "working" usually comes in the form of more shares, more replies, more direct messages than you were used to getting before.

Inbounds

The third metric is inbounds. When I talk about inbounds, I am talking about people coming to you directly, either via email or direct message. This could be people telling you they are getting value from your content, just saying hey and they wanted to share that with you. Or it could mean more inbound opportunities start coming your way: more people telling you they want to buy your product, more people inviting you to speak at events, more people asking you to be a guest on their podcast. Forget followers and engagement—this is the ultimate metric. Are more people coming to you and your business *because* you've become more visible thanks to your podcast and social media efforts? This is all relative, but it's important to call this out. Here's an example. If you are a marketing agency and you only have 117 followers on Twitter and 78 subscribers to your podcast, but your average contract is $50,000 and you've gotten three new good fit leads that came to you directly because they heard your podcast or follow you on Twitter, then you could be completely happy with 117 followers and 78 subscribers. And then you'll start thinking about what the impact of having 117,000 followers and 78,000 subscribers might be, and hopefully you'll say hey, that Dave guy was 100 percent right about me seeing the ROI of doing this podcast and being active on social media. Inbounds are similar to engagement in the sense that they are hard to perfectly measure, but I promise you you'll know when it happens (and you should tweet at me @davegerhardt when it does, by the way).

Downloads (Podcast) vs. Subscribers vs. Average Downloads

Inbounds also apply to your podcast in the same way I mentioned above. But the one metric we haven't talked about with podcasting that you should pay attention to is downloads, or how many people are listening to your podcast. This is a number that is very easy to get and you'll be able to see directly with your podcast host (e.g.,

Transistor.fm or Libsyn). Downloads are not the end goal (ideally inbounds would be the end goal; you want more people coming to you because of your podcast), but they are important to observe and benchmark. You want to see how your podcast is growing and what guests/topics your audience is most interested in. But there's a flaw in downloads: if you put out five episodes in a month, and the same 100 people download each episode, that would look like 500 downloads. But your total audience is really 100 people. This is why I like to look at downloads over a thirty-day period and then see how *that* is growing. Transistor.fm and most other hosts show this stat, but it's easy to create in either case. Many podcast hosts, including Transistor, also show you "subscribers," but I've found this number to be wildly inaccurate (this would be a measure how of how many people actually subscribe on Apple Podcasts or hit "follow" on Spotify, but I'm not sure anyone has this down to a science yet, plus many people listen to podcast episodes and never subscribe). Instead, average downloads per episode (a stat you can get in Transistor or create on your own) seems to be the best way to look at audience growth. This stat would show how well your episodes are doing seven, thirty, sixty, and ninety days after being published, and then you can benchmark that over different time periods, and as those numbers rise, you'll know you're getting more new listeners than you were before. I've also found that podcasts have a very "longtail"—meaning people will listen to them months and even years after they've been published—so short-term download numbers can be misleading.

Again, none of these metrics are worth anything unless you go and do something with them. Use these insights to guide what you go and create. This is what I mean when I say master the feedback loop. Take the insights from people (your followers) and the analytics you get from Twitter, LinkedIn, and your podcast, and match them up to keep your finger on the pulse of what people want.

It's important to state that the metrics can also be different based on your goal (and like anything, you should have a clear "why" for doing this). As a founder, if your goal in doing a podcast was to increase sales, it will be hard to measure because a direct correlation between the two is difficult to quantify, and I'd argue that starting a podcast is not the quickest path to increasing sales.

If instead, which I hope it is, you have a podcast and want to be active on social media because your goal is to build trust and credibility—which will eventually lead to more sales and growing the business—then sure, a podcast is a smart direction.

YOUR TURN

Now that I've helped set some context for how to think about social media, what to measure, and how to use the feedback loop, it's time to go and do it yourself. Start looking at your posts to see trends in responses. Do some topics get more engagement than others? What have you posted in the last week that's gotten a good response? Thirty days? Months? And the answer could be nothing. There is nothing that is getting a response. And if that's the case, there's no better time to revisit your strategy, start new, and follow what we've outlined in this book.

CONCLUSION

This book is not a guide to marketing.

It is not a guide to how to sell your product or service.

It is a guide on how to use what I've seen to be the most effective marketing tool—creating a founder brand. Hopefully this small book can achieve the ultimate goal of getting you, the founder, to become a better storyteller, start a podcast, become a publisher on social media, and use the feedback loop that building an audience can create.

Many founders will read this book. Few will actually take the advice and go and put it into play. If that's you, then you are not as far from success with podcasting and social media as you might think.

Recently, I got an email from a CEO. It said:

Just 15 months ago, I was super social media shy. Had barely 2,000 followers on LinkedIn—I wasn't posting much at all.

Until one day, my senior design manager came to me and told me, "Hey Gabe, as the CEO, you should really be more visible. Get on podcasts, share more of your thoughts on social media etc."

My response? "Nah, that's not me. I'd rather focus on building the product and our customers."

You know what he said? "Yeah but you are not doing the company any favors."

That was the impetus I needed. I took my cue from your sharing and your DGMG playbook, and started to become more active on social.

Fast forward a year, I have close to 13,000 followers on LinkedIn...

And >60% of sales calls on Gong reference—"I follow your CEO on LinkedIn and the content he's putting out."

"CEO DTC"[5] (per your words) has been a significant boost to the content that our marketing team puts out,

---

5   DTC means "Direct to Consumer."

a significant driver of demand (almost a channel by itself), and it's also great aircover for our Sales team (see Gong call below).

Thanks @Dave Gerhardt for this insight. I can attest to the power & impact of putting one's CEO out there in today's B2B environment.

That CEO built a founder brand and then used it to his advantage.

A founder brand? A brand based upon the story of the founder, and then sharing the story and the villain? A brand that solves your needs, but also gives you a human connection with a founder?

Establishing a founder brand is one marketing playbook that I recommend to any business because it works. It is *the* most effective way I have found to build a brand, create trust, and grow a business today. While it can be done with almost no financial commitment, there is a time commitment on your part as the founder and the need for consistency and dedication to the process.

And, it's fun. This model encourages you as the founder to make connections with others in your industry, find your voice, and become a leader in public. It empowers you to share your expertise and also your humanity. Being a *human* founder, with both your incredible talents and your flaws, is a much more enjoyable way to live and to build your business than the old-fashioned plan of focusing on building a *product's* brand.

The steps to building your founder brand are simple:

- Develop your story as the founder, including the backstory of what problem you are solving and why.
- Determine your niche by specifically determining your target customer. This needs to be small and very well-defined.
- Identify your villain. What problem are you solving?
- Clarify your explainer. This will allow you to be able to capture attention and start a conversation with your target audience because they can understand exactly what you are selling.
- Develop your one-liner, the one sentence that becomes your catchphrase and is sprinkled everywhere until your audience knows it by heart.

Then, the next steps involve becoming a publisher:

- Get active on social media, specifically Twitter and LinkedIn. By following my recommendations, you can be a superstar on both platforms.
- Create and release a podcast that allows you to curate your industry, share your expertise, and build a personal connection with your audience.
- Go on the road with your brand and story, sharing it at every possible public speaking event.

Finally, you need to learn to understand the feedback you get from your audience and leverage it to move your brand forward.

In each chapter, you have had a homework assignment. If you did them, you are well on your way to having a vibrant founder brand.

If you started a weekly podcast for a year right now, by next year you could have:

- Fifty-two podcast episodes,
- Fifty-two guests you've met,

- Turned that into 104 articles to help grow traffic, and
- Created 104 pieces of social content.

But maybe you weren't ready for building the whole brand yet, or you are still stuck back at determining a clear niche. Even if that is as far as you progress, you still have learned valuable information about how to build a brand. The levels in this framework allow you to grow professionally and advance as you are ready.

I wasn't trying to turn you into a marketing expert. Most of you have a product marketing team. I know better than most people how busy founders are and how many other things are on your to-do list. But if that is the situation you are in, I suggest you pick two steps or suggestions from this book and do them, and do them consistently. Maybe it will be posting daily on social media, as even that would increase the visibility of your brand.

For those of you who are committed, following the steps with fidelity, enthusiasm, an open heart and mind, and a good sense of humor, you will see that the advantage of the founder brand will take your company to the next level and keep it growing for years to come.

I wrote this book because I have seen so many great business ideas die in a coffee shop because their creators didn't know how to make them operational and how to market them. As I watched this, I wanted to share my own experience and my learnings with you. It is my hope that you will follow all three levels and reach out to me to crow about your very successful founder brand.

There are many ways to learn about marketing, and I appreciate the time you have taken to learn about it from me. I hope you will join my online community, follow me on social media, and even listen to my podcast (you can find all of that at *davegerhardt.com*). I'm doing exactly what I want you to do: I curate industry trends and news, I create new content, and I do my work in public. Sometimes you will learn about non-marketing pieces, but not often, as I stick to my recommendation of 80 percent or more of my posts being about marketing.

This is a topic near and dear to my heart, and I hope you will connect with me to share your successes or ask questions.

Your founder brand can be an amazing tool to use to build your business. Now it's time to go and make it happen. Enough reading. Time to start publishing. You'll be glad you did a year from now.

CPSIA information can be obtained
at www.ICGtesting.com
Printed in the USA
BVHW030856110222
628712BV00005B/95

9 781544 523408